Lessons
Learned

Lessons Learned

How to Negotiate the Life You Want to Live

Dr. Harris R. Cohen

abbott press®
A DIVISION OF WRITER'S DIGEST

Lessons Learned
How to Negotiate the Life You Want to Live

Abbott Press books may be ordered through booksellers or by contacting:

Abbott Press
1663 Liberty Drive
Bloomington, IN 47403
www.abbottpress.com
Phone: 1-866-697-5310

Because of the dynamic nature of the Internet, any web addresses or links contained in this book may have changed since publication and may no longer be valid. The views expressed in this work are solely those of the author and do not necessarily reflect the views of the publisher, and the publisher hereby disclaims any responsibility for them.

Any people depicted in stock imagery provided by Thinkstock are models, and such images are being used for illustrative purposes only.

Certain stock imagery © Thinkstock.

Cover Design by Phil Caminiti

ISBN: 978-1-4582-0248-2 (sc)
ISBN: 978-1-4582-0250-5 (hc)
ISBN: 978-1-4582-0249-9 (e)

Library of Congress Control Number: 2012904120

Printed in the United States of America

Abbott Press rev. date: 3/23/2012

Dedication

Although there are many people that I would like to thank for helping me become the person I am today, I especially want to acknowledge those who are nearest and dearest to me. I would like to thank my wife, Corinne; for her faith, trust, and love for me. Throughout our marriage, she has provided the inspiration and impetus for me to strive to be the best I can be.

I cherish the friendship of my son, Joshua, who has the ability to make me feel like a *real pop*! My own father was my real idol. He gave me guidance and love, and was so proud of my accomplishments.

Lastly, I would like to thank and dedicate this book to my mom. While I was growing up, she was my best friend. Mom loved me unconditionally and always supported me, even when Dad did not appear so sure of my choices! She was my lifeline to happiness because no matter how bad her health was she always had a smile on her face and beamed with love for my dad and me. I learned persistence, dedication, and how to keep a positive attitude from her.

Today, I am blessed to share my life with a wonderful wife, a great son, and two beautiful grandchildren: Nikki and Kali.

Contents

Introduction

Imagine that you are in an airport walking through an endless maze of hallways before finally reaching your gate, where you will sit for hours waiting for your plane. As you are walking, a bookshop catches your eye, and you drop in. There are hundreds of different books from which to choose. What is it that draws you to a particular book? Is it the cover, the author, the title, the pictures, the size of the book, the size of the print, the synopsis, or something else?

Human beings are vibrational in nature. In other words, we are attracted or repelled to something or someone based on a feeling. A classic example is when you meet two different people: The first person makes you feel comfortable and the second, does not. You get a good feeling with one person and a not-so-good feeling with the other. The same is true with books. Do you feel comfortable with what you've read so far? If so, please read on. By the way, you have just dealt with your first negotiation! But let's come back to that later.

Let me explain what I mean by vibrations. The expression, "If it feels good, do it," is basically the way the body is neurologically hardwired. All thought and reactions end in a feeling. It may be so fast that you cannot recognize it, but you still experience it. At birth, you are basically a clean slate of pure energy (pure vibration). As you start to learn, patterns of thought are stored in your brain. As you repeat certain patterns for periods of time, your brain puts them in compartments. Think of it as a circle. After you see, hear, taste, touch, or smell something for the first time, your brain records or "stores it vibrationally." The more you experience a particular event, the easier it is for you to experience it again.

Think of picking up a spoon for the first time. You learn how to hold it, how to use it to scoop up food, and then how to use it to bring food to your mouth. The first time you attempt this, the act is usually pretty awkward. After doing it many times, the task becomes easier and your movements more flowing. If you perform the same task repeatedly over the course of a period of time, it becomes second nature. You don't even think consciously of it.

This is how you formulate a pattern or habit. It is nothing more than repetition of the same cyclic pattern. We think in circles. Most of these patterns require little energy (vibrational energy) to be stored. However, there are some patterns that are so emotional that they are driven deep into the unconscious. These are called significant emotional events. These events require more energy to be stored than everyday events. Over the years, you may have acquired many significant emotional events; some of which you may be aware and some of which you are not aware.

As you grow and compile millions upon millions of events, your brain puts them into different categories. On a very superficial level, they formulate your personality. Remember the song from South Pacific: "You've Got to Be Taught... to hate and fear." It is true; you need to be taught these things.

From the myriad of information you have acquired from birth, you also develop a pattern of thought called decision-making. This process collects all of the available information on this one subject, and then a decision or action results. Have you ever been really upset over something and after making a decision about it you felt lighter and more centered? If so, you have just felt the release of a significant emotional event because the energy that was required to hold this in place has been released.

I experienced this phenomenon personally when I attended a seminar by Dr. Victor Frank. Dr. Frank was a chiropractor who was internationally known as a genius on vibrational healing. He spoke about a condition called "emotional dump." This is an unconscious buildup of events that can hold so much energy that they can bring a whole person down. He asked for volunteers, so I raised my hand. He said that he had never experienced a patient with more than six levels of emotional dump. However, he determined that I had *eight* layers of emotional dump. This was certainly not a contest that I had wanted to win! After performing a procedure on me, Dr. Frank asked me if I was feeling any different, and I frankly told him, "No." After all of his efforts, I felt nothing new.

So I went out to dinner, and then returned to my room to turn in early. However, upon retiring, I found that I was unable to sleep because I was so wide-awake and full of energy. Since the hotel had a twenty-four-hour gym, I worked out for about an hour and a half before I felt tired enough to go to sleep. When I awoke the next day, I felt that there had been an incredible weight lifted from my shoulders. Talk about the release of energy!

How does this all deal with negotiating a decision? Let's put what we have learned so far into action. There are few things that are more universally liked then chocolate cake. It's creamy, smooth and delicious, but fattening and filled with fat and high cholesterol. Most of us disregard the fattening and high-cholesterol part and concentrate on the creamy and delicious aspect. One day, you go to the doctor, and he tells you that you should cut down on foods that are fattening and have high cholesterol. Your first reaction is panic because chocolate cake is no longer on the menu! Nonetheless, you thank the doctor for his advice and you go about changing your diet.

One evening, you and your friends go to dinner, and they order a chocolate cake for dessert that everyone can share. Based on your experience you think the following: Should I eat some of the cake? Will one piece hurt me? How much fat and cholesterol is in a piece? You get the picture; you are left with a decision. Finally, you decide to eat the cake. However, you feel guilty after having eaten it! This is an example of negotiation because you had taken in all of the parameters, considered them, and reached a decision. Unfortunately, the decision was not in total concert with your body and, as a result, you felt guilt. If the decision had been totally acceptable by your brain, you would not have felt any guilt.

I wrote this book because I feel that the process of negotiating with oneself can be fun. I have chosen stories—some true and some not— that illustrate the negotiating process. At the end of each story, I have included "Things to Think About." My hope is to inspire you, challenge you, and maybe even make you laugh and cry. But, most of all, I want to show you how you can achieve your dreams, whether they be physical, mental, or spiritual.

Remember: "Whether you think *you can*, or you think *you can't*, you're right." Read on, and I will, as the famous author and inspirational speaker Zig Ziglar titled his book: "See You at the Top!"

Prologue

Being born with a silver spoon in your mouth or being born in abject poverty is no indicator of your destiny. How you manage to control your thought processes will determine your future. The person who makes the best choices for himself or herself is the person who gets what they want in the long run.

When we enter this world, we do so with a clean slate. We are pure energy with only a few instincts. For example, when you brush your finger across a baby's cheek, the baby will open their mouth in that direction assuming that there is food.

We learn right from wrong from our mother, father, teachers, and clergy. We move from the true vibrational, or feeling plane, to the language plane. At this point in our development, we incorporate role models. One of the most wonderful things in my life is my granddaughter. She has moved from the vibrational or straight feeling plane to the language and mimicking plane. It is absolutely hysterical to watch her try to walk exactly like her father. Imagine this adorable two-and-a-half-year-old girl walking like a six-foot, 200-pound man!

With the incorporation of language into our development, we expand our parameters of expression. We not only have to interpret what the person is saying, but also the tone—or if you will—the flavor of the conversation. In addition to the spoken word, the child also interprets body language. Let me give you an example. When I was young, my mother always used to call me Harris. When I heard that, I felt no fear. However, when I saw her with her hands on her hips and she called "Harris Roger," I was much less eager to hear what she had to say! It was not just the words that she spoke, but also the tone that she used to utter those words along with her accompanying body language that sent me the message.

As you can see, the science of human behavior is something that has fascinated me for a long time. I first became interested in this science in 1973, when I was introduced to Earl Nightingale and his recording of "The Strangest Secret." He talks about how you run your life based on your current dominant thought. Nightingale said that whatever you think about most—good or bad—would come to pass. Being much younger at the time, I was confused initially at this statement because I came to the conclusion that if that were really true, I would be *a girl!*

Now that I am older and wiser, I would like to illustrate Nightingale's theory with the following story. My father, who will always be my idol, was a very logical man. He was by far the smartest man I ever met in my life, with an incredible head for numbers. As a result, he became a Certified Public Accountant (CPA). My father's idol was his father, my grandfather, who died from diverticulitis in November of his seventy-second year. This condition affects the large intestine, which forms "out pockets." Sometimes, these pockets burst and cause infection in the gut. One such infection led to peritonitis, to which he succumbed.

My father was obsessed with the way his father died. He thought about it constantly and eventually did develop diverticulitis. It was not just fate or family history that made him a victim of this disease! One day, he was rushed to the hospital because one of these out pockets had burst and caused peritonitis. Had it not been for the medical advancement in antibiotics, my father would have died in the same month, the same year, and from the same condition that his father did! This was not a coincidence: His brain had told his body what to do. For my part, this is proof positive that what you think can affect your well being.

Armed with the knowledge that your brain can cause harm, I decided to investigate ways that the brain can help. At this point, I find it pertinent to tell you about my background. It will help you get a deeper understanding of the trials and tribulations I have overcome, and just how I overcame them. I am hoping that I can save you some frustration and pain.

I was fortunate enough to be born to two incredibly wonderful people. As I have said before, my father was a CPA. My mother was a self-made person, who by the age of fourteen had secured a job with The New York Times. Within a short time, she became a feature writer for the Times. She enjoyed a career there for more than twenty years years. Both of them were career people and, as such, did not think too much of marriage.

However, both my parents spent weekends in the Catskills and loved golf. One weekend, my father and mother were paired in a foursome. During the play of eighteen holes, they found that they had lots in common. My mother lived in an apartment building in New York City with her brother, Nat. My father lived in an apartment building in New York City with his brother, Nat. In fact, they lived in the very same apartment building for years and had never run into each other! It took golf in the Catskills to get them together!

With two career people, marriage seemed out of the question. The plan was for them to just be friends. My father was very happy with his practice, and he was also involved with his other brothers in a furniture business, coincidently named Harris Cohen and Sons. My mother was engrossed in her career. She was even invited to one of the inaugural balls of President Franklin Delano Roosevelt and met Eleanor Roosevelt at the affair.

Nonetheless, while they were together on a trip to Florida, my father popped the question, and my mother said, "Yes," before he could finish the sentence! So, on August 18, 1941, my parents were married. All was well in the Cohen household until December 7, 1941. At thirty-six years old, my father never thought that he would be drafted into the U.S. Army. Boy, was he wrong! He was inducted into the Army shortly after January of 1942.

My mother, with all her connections, was able to find out where my father was going to be stationed. She immediately left The New York Times so that she could be with him. As luck would have it, he was stationed in New Mexico. His background as a CPA made him the logical candidate to run the office at Kirkland field in Albuquerque, New Mexico. My parents spent the war years together, traveling, and basically enjoying each other. However, there was something missing: children!

On August 22, 1946, my mother and father were blessed with a bouncing baby boy (me). To quote my mother: "It was your father's last burst of energy." I would be the one and only child: No brothers, no sisters, just me! My singular status enabled me to see up close and personal how well two people could get along. I never saw them fight. I only saw abounding love between them. I had the greatest formative years that anyone could have wished for.

The only downside was that my life experience was only with older people. Socializing with children my own age was a different story. Remember, this was before nursery school or daycare! Since I had no real experience with other young children on a consistent basis, I had a very difficult time relating to my peers. To make matters worse, I was fat and had a tendency to cry a lot. This was a recipe for real psychological trouble.

Academically, I was bright, but never really applied myself. My parents told me that I could do anything that I wanted to do as long as I went to college. However, I did not want to go to college because I thought it would be even worse than high school where I was teased mercilessly. Nonetheless, I did attend college and graduated with a major in biology. I always wanted to be a doctor, but was unable to follow that dream at that time.

I graduated from college in 1968. Since there was a shortage of educators, I decided to become a teacher. I taught junior high school science for three years and found that I really loved it. I moved on to teach high school for another three years, where I taught advanced biology and chemistry. I really enjoyed the challenge and rewards of teaching. However, my dream to be a doctor remained unfulfilled.

In 1975, I was given the opportunity to become a pharmaceutical salesman. I jumped at the chance because I thought it would get me closer to my ultimate goal. I did extremely well as a pharmaceutical rep, but was bored and very unhappy. I did not like the way I was treated by the physicians and swore that if I ever became a doctor, I would never treat people the way that they did!

The chance to pursue my dream came when my brother-in-law (at the time) began attending chiropractic college. He asked me if I would like to go, but I told him that I did not want to be a quack! (At that time, chiropractors were not looked upon as real doctors.) After his first year, I started to consider the offer more seriously. I figured that if I was a good salesman. I could sell myself as a chiropractor. After all, I would have Dr. in front of my name and that was my goal. So, in September of 1976, I enrolled in chiropractic college.

The next four years were extremely interesting. I went to school from eight in the morning to three in the afternoon. Then, I did my detail work for the pharmaceutical company until approximately eight in the evening. After I did that, I went home and studied for about three hours, slept for four hours, and beginning at approximately five in the morning, I visited hospitals. By the way, I was also a paramedic on the weekends. To say life was hectic is an understatement!

During this time, my ex-wife broke the news that she was pregnant with our second child. Joshua was born on September 16, 1977. Unfortunately, Joshua had problems from birth and had grand-mal seizures. The doctors were very concerned and also told us that he might be retarded. His seizures were bad and would not stop, so he was given lots of drugs to no avail. About three days later, Joshua developed congestive heart failure and the doctors held out little hope for his survival. Poor Josh had not put out urine for seven hours and was literally poisoning himself from the inside out.

When I received the bad news, I was at chiropractic college. The doctors back at the hospital advised me: "Come see your son before he dies." I asked a professor at the school: "What I should do?" (Remember we are talking about grand-mal seizures and possible retardation.) The wise professor looked at me and said: "Adjust the child and miracles will happen." I looked at him straight in the eye and told him that he was full of, well, fecal matter. The professor said: "You really are a good salesman." I glared at him with a strange look and said: "What does that have to do with anything?" He said: "You can fool other people about your belief, but you really can't fool yourself. If you think chiropractic *does not work*, you are right; and if you think it *does work*, you are also right."

The professor continued: "What do you have to lose by doing an adjustment on your three-day-old child?" In desperation, I asked him what I should do. He said: "Wiggle his Atlas!" In my head, I said: "Yeah, that's really scientific!" Nonetheless, I took his advice, and I set off to the hospital to adjust my three-day-old child. During the ride to the hospital, I reviewed what my choices were.

On one hand, my paramedic training dictated that I follow the protocol of medicine. This would mean medicating Josh throughout his childhood. I knew that this type of medication would slow his cognitive or thinking processes and would probably exacerbate or make worse the possible consequences of his mental retardation.

On the other hand, what if I embrace the non-traditional protocol that the chiropractic professor had proposed? This protocol indicated that I should: "Wiggle his Atlas." The basic philosophy of chiropractic is to normalize the nervous system by removing irritation caused by misaligned vertebrae. This philosophy made sense to me. So, I decided to put my faith and belief in my new profession, which meant adjusting my three-day-old child. Having come to this conclusion, I reviewed exactly what I was to do.

When I arrived at the hospital, I went straight to the neo-natal intensive care unit. There was my son, naked and crying. I picked him up, put my hand on his neck and proceeded to "Wiggle his Atlas!" As

I did, I said to him: "Josh. This one's for you!" Within ten minutes, his seizures stopped! His color changed, and he started to move. Three days later, he was discharged from the hospital and has been seizure-free for more than thirty years. (By the way, he's also very intelligent and has earned a degree from Stony Brook University.)

As a result of my careful thought process, I reached a reasonable conclusion that may have saved my son's life. The art of negotiation that we are going to explore in this book is making good choices based on good sound advice and experience. One of the largest challenges in life is to gain control over your own thinking. Remember, in most cases no one can make you feel, do, or act in any way without your own permission.

How to Read This Book

Some books are meant to be read as a means of recreation. Others are read for the content they possess. Still others are read as a blueprint for growth.

I envision people reading this material as a combination of each of the above. I recommend that you read over the material once to get a general picture of the process. Then, go through the first six section headings, and pick out an area that you would like to work on. Read the section you have selected, and then at the end of each, look over the "Things to Think About." Once you feel that you have grasped the overall concept of each section, move on to another section. After you have read all six of the sections and you have completed all of the "Things to Think About," you are now ready to formulate a plan for your future successes using the process in the seventh and final section: "Goals."

As you read, I hope that you enjoy the journey on your way to achieving success.

SECTION ONE

Who Am I?

"Know thyself means this, that you get acquainted with what you know, and what you can do."

Menander

Greek Comic Dramatist

Tom

Here was this six-foot tall, 200-pound adolescent walking towards me ready to rip my head off. In my most commanding voice, I told him to: "Sit down!" He did, and I breathed a sigh of relief. He could have squashed me like a grape! Little did I know then that this large person would teach me a large lesson in life.

My first occupation was teacher of biology, chemistry, and general science. Although I was fortunate to teach advanced classes in regents biology, I was also assigned one class in physical science. This class in physical science was reserved for students who just needed a credit in science to get a high-school diploma. These students were a drastic change from the other young adolescents that I had been teaching.

This particular class was a real challenge. The students didn't want to learn and had no interest in the course whatsoever. The most you could hope for was to keep their attention, making it possible for them to learn *something*. One day, I decided that we would just read aloud from the textbook. Each one of the students took their turn until it came to Tom. He looked at me with his steely gray eyes, and said: "I'm not reading from the book."

I had learned that confrontation was not a good way to motivate someone, but my education and experience were lost in the moment. My retort was: "What do you have for a brain?" He stared me down even more intently, and again said: "I'm not reading from the book." I took this as a challenge (oh, how dumb!) and told him: "If you don't read from the book, there will be consequences!" He stood up, came towards me, and screamed: "I'm going to leave, and I'm never coming back!" To that, I commanded: "Sit down!" He did, and I was very relieved. As I mentioned before, he was a big guy and could have squashed me like a grape!

After the class was over, I talked with him. I apologized for embarrassing him in front of his fellow students. He accepted my apology and proceeded to tell me about himself. Although he appeared to be slow, this adolescent had an IQ in the 140s, which is genius level. However, he was severely dyslexic. In fact, Tom was so bright that he was able to go from kindergarten to sixth grade before anyone realized that he might be dyslexic. Even after the diagnosis had been determined, no real measures were taken in order to combat the condition.

As a result, Tom became extremely disgruntled about school and about life. If it were not for the fact that he loved to work with his hands and that his father had gotten him into carpentry, Tom probably would have wound up in serious trouble or even incarcerated! Luckily, his superior intellect enabled him to overcome his handicap. He learned to transpose numbers when necessary and became an exceptional carpenter.

I found Tom's story fascinating, and throughout the school year we grew closer. I was moving into a new house and discussed with him what sort of countertops I should use in the kitchen. He came up with some really great ideas.

The end of the year arrived, and it was almost time for Tom to graduate. The high school where I taught was also a vocational school. Tom spent the morning in the academic portion of the high school and then, the afternoon in the vocational portion. Each year, the carpentry school would literally build a house from scratch. This included the walls, the interior, and the electric. The house was complete except for the foundation. As a result of his work on the house, Tom received the Outstanding Senior Award for Carpentry. This couldn't have happened to a nicer kid!

The only thing that would prevent Tom from pursuing his budding carpentry career was the lack of a driver's license. But he was determined. So off to the DMV he went, to get a Learner's Permit. Although he could not read the test because of his dyslexia, Tom was assigned a proctor who would give this "poor dumb boy" the test.

4

Much to everyone's surprise, Tom got 100 percent! No dumb kid here! So, armed with his new Learner's Permit, and soon, his high school diploma, Tom was happy and secure in his future for the first time. What a sight to see! Talk about the importance of self-esteem!

Near the end of the school year, Tom asked me to come around to the back of the vocational school. As I approached the back of the school, I saw Tom holding a very large piece of wood. He told me that this was the chopping block for which I'd been searching. It was three foot by six foot and was four inches thick of solid oak. This chopping block was hand doweled and varnished with fourteen coats. There wasn't even one piece of metal in it! This masterpiece had been made simply by piecing wood together and gluing it. It was indeed the perfect chopping block (about three hundred pounds worth)! He said that this was his gift to me for taking the time to get to know him better. With tears running down my cheeks, I accepted the chopping block with open arms. In fact, this wonderful gift remained part of my home until we sold my first house fifteen years later.

Teaching is a wonderful profession because you can influence young people in a positive direction. Sometimes, the role is reversed. Although I taught Tom many things, he taught me so much more! He taught me how to be tolerant of other people. In situations where people might use their fists, Tom taught me to turn the other cheek and laugh. He made me understand what it was like to be handicapped, when few people other than the handicapped understood. Basically, he taught me how to be a better human being!

As you think about this story, keep in mind all of the prejudices that people exhibit every day, ranging from prejudice regarding the color of people's skin to the way people talk. What is prejudice? The answer to that is simply ignorance. When I embarrassed him, Tom knew that it was smarter for him to sit down than it was to confront me. At seventeen-and-a-half years old, this adolescent realized that it was prejudice (my ignorance of his condition)—not any maliciousness on my part—that caused me to say what I did. How enlightened Tom is!

Things to Think About

Think of something that you might have a prejudice against.

- What is the basis of that prejudice?
- What factors would cause you to change your perception?
- Would these changes be beneficial to you?

A great example of this concept would be for you to try a food that you don't like.

- Why don't you like it? (Was it the smell or the consistency?)
- What would it take for you to change your opinion?
- If you tried it and you liked it, would you then eat it on a consistent basis?

In order for you to make changes, have fun in the process. If you make it a game, the task seems lighter, can be more appealing, and therefore easier for you to execute.

Transformations

It was a brisk autumn day, as I walked from the science building to the athletic center. The sun was shining, and there wasn't a cloud in the sky. I felt good about myself and what I had done over the past six months to transform my body. As I passed several classmates, one girl told me how good I looked. This put a spring in my step because that idea had never been part of my internal representation to that point. It was truly a defining moment in my life!

Let me take you back a few years. As an only child, I was the love of my parents' life and could do no wrong. I could get anything that I wanted, included anything and everything to eat that I wanted! Apparently, my mother knew little about nutrition or good eating habits. Over my childhood years, I became quite overweight. Regardless, my mother had always told me that I was "a beautiful boy!" However, I was receiving mixed messages: my parents said I was beautiful, but my peers said I was a fat kid. The more the kids baited me and called me fat, the more miserable I felt. So, I tried to relieve that misery by turning to food. Nonetheless, I still seemed to have the approval of my parents regarding my physical form. I became really conflicted: Was I a fat kid or was I a beautiful boy?

I am sure you can understand the battle that was going on inside my head during my childhood and adolescent years. There was a constant struggle within my brain over whether I was fat, which meant I was unworthy of my peers' friendship, or whether I was beautiful and a person that attracted others. To compensate for the lack of friendship, companionship, and socialization with my peers, I became very comfortable hanging around people my parents' age. I found they were less judgmental and accepted me for what I was: a fat kid who always hung around his parents! Quite honestly, I just found it much easier to socialize with older people than with people my own age.

I vividly remember my seventh and eighth grade years, especially my first day of class in seventh grade. I had gotten a belt, which did not secure in the usual way. It was one of those belts where one piece fits into the other. When it was closed, the belt had a slight raised button on the belt buckle. As I walked into the building, one of my classmates touched the button on top of my belt. He said: "If I touch your pressure gauge, will all the gas come out?" As the rumor of this incident circulated, the ridicule just did not stop. All of the other kids climbed on the bandwagon. It upset me so much that I told my parents about it. They took it seriously enough to send me to a psychologist for fear that I would do something drastic!

The psychologist was a brilliant man. His advised me to ignore the kids that were teasing me and eventually they would give up. I can remember distinctly going back to science class and looking at all of those kids. I realized I should ignore all of them, but I simply couldn't do it. However, as time passed, the uniqueness of teasing me got old, and they finally stopped. You can imagine how my self-esteem and self-image were affected by all of this!

As I neared the completion of my high-school experience, I found it most gratifying that I could literally start anew at college. When I arrived at college, I was five-foot seven-inches tall, but I weighed two hundred pounds. Despite my average height, I was a *big boy!* Soon it was apparent that I was not going to fare any better there because I had also arrived equipped with the same brain. My brain had stored all of the bad information and experience that I had gathered during my earlier childhood and adolescence. My frame of reference was that of a fat kid who usually began to cry when confronted. After all, I had been teased unmercifully. I had physically changed my environment, but mentally I retained the same frame of reference.

At college, things took a turn for the worse. After the first semester, I was the only one who had a single room because nobody wanted to room with me. Don't get me wrong: I was meticulous in my personal hygiene and was pretty neat—for a guy! However, I wanted friends so desperately that I smothered them and as a result most of my classmates stayed away. Have you heard that when God closes a door, he leaves a window open? My window was my singing voice. I had received scholarship offers, and now, as a freshman, I got into the concert college choir. For the first time, I was a member of a group and really enjoyed it. However, after a short period of time, the same things began to happen with the choir that had happened to me all my life before. Something needed to change!

As part of the choir, we toured the entire Northeast. By my sophomore year, I was the tenor soloist. We would usually perform an average of two concerts per day for fourteen days. All we did was eat, sleep, and sing! You can imagine how grueling those fourteen days were! My parents had bought me a new suit for the choir tour. The waist on the pants was 44 inches. Unfortunately, by the end of choir tour, I must have gained a lot of weight because I was unable to button my pants. To be exact, I had added sixteen pounds, ballooning my weight to a whopping 216 pounds! I had a forty-four-inch chest and a forty-four-inch waist, so I look like a large barber pole. I was so unhappy: I had reached bottom.

I decided to go home for the remainder of Spring Break. I would be in a safe place, with my parents at our house, confident that nobody could tease me there. While at home and rummaging through my old clothes, I found my old Boy Scout shorts. During my Boy Scout days (age eleven), I had a thirty-four-inch waist. My mother told me to put them on, just to see how much I'd grown. After attempting to put the shorts on, I found that the waistband was approximately ten inches too small. As I showed my mother this humongous gap between the clasp and the button on the shorts, my father (who was my idol) walked in. He looked at me and said that I had the fattest damn ass he had ever seen in his life! Talk about being crushed! The man I admired most in all of the world, the smartest man I had ever met, just told me that I had a *really fat ass.* Something needed to be done!

Back at school, I made up my mind to change. Changing is difficult because you must literally negotiate with your prior experiences and frame them in a way that will serve you more positively in the future. I immediately focused on my weight. I decided to go on a zero-carbohydrate diet. I tried this for approximately two weeks and discovered that when my brain was deprived of carbohydrates for such a period, I became a raging lunatic! This obviously was not the route to take to accomplish my weight loss and physical change. Then, I decided to try eating one meal a day. (At the time, this was considered okay, but we know now that this is not the best choice for weight-loss.) I did that for sixteen weeks. In addition, I embarked on a jogging program, and discovered that I enjoyed physical exercise a lot. At the end of the sixteen weeks, I had lost sixty pounds and had reduced my waist from forty-four inches to thirty-two inches!

By the way, most college students don't go clothes shopping during the middle of the semester. After I started to lose weight, my pants became too large for me. But, instead of buying new pants, I folded the pants over and then wore a belt to hold everything in place. Unfortunately, at a glance, this arrangement made my pants look as if my fly were constantly open! To be honest, I was totally unaware of that.

My parents came up to college to take me back home for the summer. There, I was going to be a lifeguard for the first time. My mother hadn't seen me in sixteen weeks and didn't recognize me! On the other hand, my father just looked at me and smiled (talk about elation on my part—Daddy's approval). After we arrived home, the first thing my parents did was take me down to the local clothing shop to pick up some pants so I didn't look like I had my fly open all the time!

Talk about a life changing experience! I had the best time of my life that summer. I was a lifeguard: thin, in good shape, and for the first time, truly happy. What enabled me to make this transformation? Was it physical or was it mental? The correct answer to that question: It was both!

When you change your internal representation, you change yourself. Most people who lose weight gain it back within five years. On the other hand, I have kept the weight off for forty-two years and counting! This is certainly a testament to my internal ability to change and my acceptance of that change.

At this point in my life, I am calm and content as well as truly happy. I am able to make choices now based on my knowledge, experience, and faith in myself. I have learned to listen to my inner voice. I make a choice—not out of emotion or what other people say or want—but based on what I think is in my best interest at the time. Remember, you are in a constant state of change, so listening to your inner voice is very important.

I know you've heard this before, but I really believe if *I* can do it, *you* can do it! Go for it.

Be the person you truly want to be. The power to change is all between your two ears!

Things to Think About

Think of something that you would like to change about yourself.

- What would this change look like, sound like, taste like, feel like, and smell like?
- Make a detailed list of the steps you would need to make this change possible.
- Now think of how you will feel when this change has occurred. Use all of your senses to make this internal picture as real as possible.
-
- Keep these feelings in mind for as long as you can and repeat these procedures constantly. The repetition of envisioning what you want speeds the change process along.

Good luck in changing!

Self-Esteem Negotiation

It's important to find commonality between you and the patient, according to the doctor that spoke at a seminar that I had attended. He advised that we look for a way to compliment our patients. It made sense to me to find some common ground between the patient and the doctor. After all, a sincere compliment would break the ice, relax the patient, and make the patient feel like the doctor was interested not only in the patient's condition, but also the patient as a whole person.

After my return home and arrival at the office, I held a real powwow with my staff. I explained to them that we really needed to find something in each of our patients that we could earnestly compliment them on. I told them I didn't really care if it was related to their health, their clothes, their jewelry, or something else. As the meeting progressed, I started to go over the patient list with the staff. We began to visualize just how we might be able to compliment each patient. Most of them were easy because they possessed many positive aspects for which they could be honestly complimented. Then, of course, there were the chosen few! Concerning these folks, you had to think hard and long before you could find a positive thing on which to comment.

One such patient, I will call Mrs. Green Teeth, simply because *she had green teeth!* Honestly, those suckers look liked they had not been brushed since she was a kid! To round out the picture, she was approximately five-foot two-inches tall and probably weighed 350 pounds. In order to cover her girth, she always wore a tent-like dress. In addition to her off-putting physical appearance, she also had really bad body odor. It was so bad that after her treatments, we had to literally fumigate the adjusting room.

As we came upon Mrs. Green Teeth's name, I looked blankly at my staff and my staff looked blankly back! We all seemed to draw a collective deep sigh; while saying to ourselves, there must be something we can compliment this lady on! All of a sudden, it came to me: "What about her hair?" One of them shouted: "You're right! Her hair always looks great!" All of the eyes in the room lit up. We had found it!

Okay, let me set the scene. My office is located in a shopping center and has a glass storefront. As patients get out of their cars, we can see who is coming. So, here's what we planned. When Mrs. Green Teeth was approaching the office, I would go into the back and suck on some oxygen so I would be able to hold my breath long enough to adjust her without having to breathe. (Just kidding!) After greeting her, I would tell Mrs. Green Teeth that her hair looks great, place her down on the adjusting table, and adjust her low back. Then, I would ask her to turn over. While she was struggling to do that, I would leave the room and go into the hallway where I could hyperventilate! (Again, just kidding!) Then, I would return and do her neck, while holding my breath. Once she was fully adjusted, I would usher her out, grab a large can of air refresher and fumigate the room. (Really!)

The stage was set. On the appointed day, at the appointed time, Mrs. Green teeth pulled into the parking lot. The staff was on high alert. As Mrs. Green teeth approached, our noses warned us that she was coming! She opened the door, walked in, and with much enthusiasm, a few of the staff said in concert: "Your hair looks really nice today." Then, one of them ushered her into an adjusting room.

Then, I greeted Mrs. Green Teeth and also complimented her on her hair. I placed her on the adjustment table and proceeded to adjust her low back. Then, I asked her to turn over. While she was doing it, I went outside to re-oxygenate myself. When I returned, I adjusted her neck and then sent her on her way. Immediately after her exit, we fumigated the room.

After Mrs. Green Teeth's visit, I asked my staff how they think we did. All of them were satisfied with our performance and the reaction. For the rest of the day, we made sure to compliment each and every person that came in the door. Doing this made us feel good and made our patients feel good. The results were so outstanding that we decided to make it a habit in my practice.

Two days later, Mrs. Green Teeth was scheduled for another appointment. The staff and I were poised to go into action. I was to run for the back, and they were to compliment her on her hair. However, as soon as she entered the office, she asked to speak the members of my staff and me. I'm sure you can appreciate the amount of panic that I felt in that moment. As I pictured her filing a lawsuit, all those long years of study I endured coursed through my head. To my joy and surprise, she said: "I would like to thank you for giving me back my self-esteem."

All of us were dumbfounded. Mrs. Green Teeth explained that she especially appreciated it because we really did not know her. Of course, that was true. She told us that her husband and children verbally abuse her on a consistent basis. Since she had gotten pregnant, she had married the father right out of high school. From that moment on, her husband verbally abused her. He complained about her weight, her attitude, and everything else. When her children got old enough to understand what Dad was doing, they joined in and laid it on even more.

Mrs. Green Teeth said that when she was in high school, she had been an average student. The one thing that she excelled at was hairdressing, and she had wanted so much to become a hairdresser. Her aspirations were shattered when she found out she was pregnant. Through the years she had thought many times about going back to school, but her low self-esteem from all the abuse prevented her from doing so. This situation led to her weight gain and lack of personal hygiene, which was her way of fighting back at her husband and children. Under these conditions, they didn't dare get close to her. What a story!

With just a little boost from a few compliments on her hair, Mrs. Green Teeth was able to realize that she was a person who mattered. Somebody had noticed her and had said something nice. Over the next few weeks, her teeth became whiter and whiter, and her hygiene improved until she was downright pleasant to be around. Now when Mrs. White Teeth walks into the office, we have to hold back from applauding. What an ending!

Have you ever run into a person like the former Mrs. Green Teeth? You never know what a nice word or kind gesture from you will do. It's much better to compliment somebody on something than tell them: "You really look tired today." What possible good could that do! What words of encouragement can you give to someone today? What way can you make this day a better day for you and people around you? If you keep these ideas in mind, you might help other people and yourself to be happier.

Things to Think About

Although the story above illustrates how to build self-esteem in other people, this exercise is designed to build self-esteem in you. Look in the mirror. Are you happy with the image that looks back at you? Now look into your own eyes: Do they exhibit confidence? If they don't, try the following.

- Each day, as you look into the mirror, imagine the person that you want to be. Notice what changes take place. Do you look different? Does that new image make you feel different? If the answer is yes, practice visualizing this person each time that you look at yourself in the mirror.

Eventually, the new image will become reality.

SECTION TWO

Science of Negotiations

"Always do your best. What you plant now, you will harvest later."

Augustine "Og" Mandino, II
Famous American Author

How Do It Know?

A guy walks into a department store and walks up to the clerk and asks to buy a thermos. He picks one out, pays for it, and walks out of the store. The next day the guy walks back into the store and demands to see the manager. He meets the manager and tells him that he's totally dissatisfied with the thermos. The manager asks him why. The guy says: "When I fill the thermos up with something cold the liquid remains cold, and when I fill the thermos with something hot the liquid stays hot." The manager looks at the man quizzically and says: "That's the function of a thermos." Apparently confused, the man looks back at him and says: "I don't understand. How do it know?"

Although I think this story is really cute, I shared it because it leads to a much more interesting subject: How does the brain really work? How are you able to breathe? How are you able to read? How are you able to catch a baseball? How are you able to perform the countless actions that sustain our very existence? In other words, when it comes to the brain: "How do it know?"

Think of the brain as a complex network of telephone lines. Each line goes to a specific place. You may have more than one line going to any one particular place. In other words, the more complicated the action, the more lines that are dedicated to produce the result. That only makes sense, doesn't it? On a very superficial level, this explains how people who have had brain injuries recover because only parts of their brains were damaged. We all have an abundance of lines dedicated to any one function.

The nervous system sort of looks like a really large jellyfish. You have the large body, which is the brain, and millions upon millions of tentacles coming out from it, which are the nerves. These nerves go to pretty much every cell in your body. The way these nerves transmit impulses is through electricity. That's why when you go to the doctor and he wants to test your heart, he uses an EKG (electrocardiogram) machine.

So, if the nerves run on electricity that moves through them constantly, the electricity is always on. If that's the case, you might ask: "How come they do not burn out?" The reason is that there are gaps at certain points along these nerves. Within these gaps, special chemicals are stimulated that cause the electrical impulse to pass over the gap.

My granddaughter loves the television show, "Dora the Explorer." One of the characters is a grumpy old man. He guards the bridge and will not let anyone cross over. The only way you can cross over is to answer a riddle. Think of the gap between the nerve endings as the bridge and the grumpy old man as the chemicals. When you answer the riddle correctly, the grumpy old man lets you cross over the bridge. When the impulse comes to the end of the nerve, the chemicals are released, and the impulse can continue.

You have in your body millions upon millions of nerves. These nerves convey electrical impulses to all the cells in your body. They do this in a circular pattern. Everything you think, feel, or move is the result of a circular pattern. Even reflexes are circular in nature. There is always a starting point, a midpoint that is either the brain or spinal cord, and an endpoint that is the reaction. Decision-making is no exception to this rule. The art of negotiating with yourself is your ability to break the cyclical pattern and change it. Once you have done this, a new conclusion can be drawn.

Let me give you an example in the art of self-negotiation. Overeating is epidemic in this country. It is an example of a bad habit. Habits are formed by repetitive movements until they become unconscious in nature. To break a habit, one needs a so-called pattern interruption. In this case, you need to break the cyclical pattern of unconscious eating. A good example of a pattern interrupt is to put a sign on your refrigerator that says: "Why are you eating this?" The process is now stopped, and then a new decision can be made. This is an example of internal negotiations. The decision-making is intellectual. The final check is both intellectual and feeling.

The more conscious you are of how you think and what you think about, the more of your actions will emanate from choice versus habit. This is the way to achieve a consciously directed life!

Things to Think About

Choose a habit. It could be something small or large. Now write down the following:

- What is the trigger? In other words, what starts the reaction?
- What is the resulting action, and what is the ultimate end product of that action?
- When did you realize you were repeating a habit? Are you aware of the process you went through to reach this action?
-

Now do the task consciously, making sure that you are aware of each step that you take to perform the task. By breaking down a habit into its component parts, you will be able to change the outcome and not do the task in the same way again. Then, it is a choice, not merely a habit.

Just Ease Off the Clutch

Imagine a vacant parking lot with padded light poles, an extremely nervous first-time driver behind the wheel and an even more nervous parent sitting in the passenger seat. To make matters worse, imagine the car with a stick shift (not an automatic transmission). The ever-so-patient parent says: "Okay, just ease off on the clutch and give it a little bit of gas." After both of their heads bounce back from the headrests, the parent—who is now struggling to remain calm—asks the young person to try it again and this time, with the foot not so heavy on the gas! Have you got the picture? If you drive a car and have ever given lessons to or received lessons from a family member, you have probably experienced this in one form or another.

This analogy will go a long way to explain to you how we acquire, put into logical order, and retain information. The more we do a task, the more proficient we become at doing that task. The more proficient we become at the task, the less conscious awareness we need to do the task. This may sound confusing, so let's break it down into four steps.

The first step is that you are *unconsciously incompetent*. In other words, you don't know that you don't know. In the case of driving, let's consider a young person about to drive a car for the first time. They haven't the foggiest idea how to drive. All they know is that after they get in, the car takes them where they want to go.

The second step is that you are *consciously incompetent*. You know you don't know how to drive the car. You are certainly aware that it is used for transportation, but you are unaware of the physical requirements necessary to drive the car. You are concerned that you may not know the difference between the break pedal and the gas pedal!

The third step is that you are *consciously competent*. This is your parent's worst nightmare! You are now aware of how to drive the car and are competent enough with the mechanics of driving that you were awarded a driver's license. However, you need to be aware of all the different aspects of driving. For example, you must keep in mind that you need to look in the rearview mirror, turn your head side-to-side at intersections, and slow down when approaching a stop sign.

The fourth and final step is that you are *unconsciously competent*. This means that you have practiced all of the intricacies of driving and have mastered them. Without much thought, you look in the rearview mirror, turn your head side-to-side at intersections, and slow down when approaching a stop sign. Rather than conscious actions, these have become unconscious actions. (You just do it!)

Your brain learns information the same way, by repetition. The more you do a task, the easier it becomes. How do you know if you are doing the task in the right way? Most people say that when they do something right, it feels right to them. This is the truth, the whole truth, and nothing but the truth! Your feelings run your life. Any choice that you make from brushing your teeth to deciding what you will eat ends in a feeling. The feeling may be so fleeting that you may not be able to recognize it, but the feeling still occurred. When we learn a new task and it is done correctly, we are satisfied with the results. As the drill sergeant said to the soldier: "If you do it right in practice, you'll do it right in combat, son."

To make a decision about something, one must have knowledge of the situation, experience with the situation (this may be real or by simulation), and understanding of the proposed outcome. In other words, a decision is based upon numerous choices. These choices are your negotiating tools. In as little as a split second, you may have to weigh the options, come to a decision, and (if it feels good) conclude the process with action.

A good example of split-second internal negotiations is an

outfielder's attempt to catch a fly ball. He must calculate the speed and trajectory of the ball, the distance he has to travel to catch the ball, and how fast he will have to run to get there. Those decisions, or internal negotiations, are made easier by repetition. (In baseball, talent helps, too.) Generally, the more you practice, the easier decisions become. Ask any baseball star!

Things to Think About

In your experience, there must have been times when you had to memorize something quickly.

- Go back to that time and try to repeat the steps that you took in order to remember the piece. It's not important what you memorized, only how you memorized it. The process that you used to memorize the material is a sterling example of the art of internal negotiations.
- In order to memorize something one must go through a particular set of steps. Each step is a negotiating tool to your final destination, which is memorizing the piece. Once this idea of choice is firmly instilled within you, your brain will stop thinking about weeds (negative thoughts) and instead grow beautiful flowers (positive thoughts).
- Another good example of this process is learning a new dance step. You go through the steps slowly at first. As you get more familiar with the steps, you speed them up to the correct tempo. Soon you will be able to perform the steps without thinking.

You literally negotiated each dance.

The Hurricane

I saw in front of me a man of seventy years or more who had the enthusiasm and heart of a true winner. The man appeared old on the outside, but it was also apparent that on the inside, he held a zeal for the blessing of life. This man sat with us and had us spellbound with his experience of life. Rubin "Hurricane" Carter, LLD, was a former middleweight boxer who had been wrongly accused of murder and spent twenty-two years in prison. To listen to Dr. Carter was to listen to pearls of wisdom.

My wife and I frequently vacation in Jamaica. On one of our more recent trips, we stayed at a resort on the south side of the island. We were in the dining area when someone asked us if we had ever heard of Rubin Carter (who was also eating there). My father was a boxing aficionado and had told me a lot of stories about famous boxers. Rubin Carter was high on his list because Carter had been a top-ranked middleweight who was considered a contender for the middleweight title. Unfortunately, he was imprisoned before the bout was arranged. I went up to Dr. Carter and introduced my wife and myself. He was gracious and seemed interested in getting to know us better. This was certainly not the usual *modus operandi* of celebrities.

For hours, Dr. Carter and his friend Tom sat with us telling tales of his experiences. He had been a top-ranked middleweight boxer before he got convicted of murder and sentenced to life imprisonment. Life was over, as he had known it.

Dr. Carter's youth was troubled to say the least. He was in and out of it most of the time. He entered the armed forces where his skill of boxing became well known. He served as a paratrooper and was discharged. After returning to his hometown of Patterson, New Jersey, he was harassed by the local police. For some reason, one particular detective was most interested in making Dr. Carter's life miserable. After one of Dr. Carter's fights, he was allegedly in a bar and a triple murder took place. He was arrested, convicted of murder, and sent to prison.

Knowing that he did not commit this murder and was falsely accused made Dr. Carter more resentful than a guilty man might have been. He entered prison and was rebellious. He was the recipient of many unthinkable physical and psychological experiences. He rebelled against all of it. At some point in his incarceration, Dr. Carter made a conscious decision to turn his life into a search for the truth. This included the truth about the murder. To be exonerated from the murder charge, Dr. Carter realized he would have to be knowledgeable and present compelling evidence that would earn him a new trial. He was able to gather support for his new trial. Such celebrities as Mohammed Ali and others came to his aid. He was awarded a new trial, tried a second time, and unfortunately found guilty again.

Faced with the daunting task of arranging for another trial was too much for the former middleweight contender. He had had great support from people and yet was convicted a second time. Who would listen to him? Who would believe him? What should he do? According to Rubin, he kept his resolve and was determined to exonerate himself. He knew he could never do it alone.

When one has faith and belief that the truth will come out, one is never truly lost. Dr. Carter had that faith and belief, and, as a result of that, he is now a free man. He is the first to tell you that faith in justice and belief in a higher being are the only things that keep people going. He also feels that he was chosen to go through this experience to help others who were less fortunate than he.

To have spent time with Rubin Carter was a real highlight of my life. I learned from him that the choices that we make change constantly depending on our outlook or goal. When we look at the situation from a negative point of view, we can only draw negative conclusions. On the other hand, when we face the situation with a positive outcome in mind, miracles can happen. To listen to Dr. Carter speak is to be reminded that you can be the best that you can be if you give yourself the opportunity.

Rubin Carter is now helping others who were wrongly accused become exonerated. Although he is not the imposing figure that he once was, his message is as powerful as any punch delivered to an opponent. His message of hope, faith, persistence, and determination are present with each word that he speaks.

I tell this story because it is a true example in the art of negotiating with oneself. Dr. Carter could have just given up when he was wrongly accused. He could have turned into another jailhouse guy. He could have continued to fight and buck the system. He could have done all of those things, but he chose to look for the positive and set specific outcomes for himself. He looked towards the future, took into consideration all of the options, and chose carefully. As the conditions changed, so did his outcomes. In other words, he was not fixed on a specific set of action steps, but was able to become flexible in his thinking processes.

Twenty-two years is a long time to keep your eyes fixed on the prize. My hat is off to Rubin Carter, who will always have my great respect and admiration.

Things to Think About

The concept of negotiating with yourself is not new. You do it all the time but most the time you do it unconsciously.

- Pick one goal or outcome that you would like to achieve. Please make the goal relatively easy to achieve because I want you to succeed.
- Make a list of all of the rewards that you will get from achieving this goal. Now put a priority on one of those rewards.
- List what you would see, hear, taste, touch, and smell if you achieved this goal.
- • Then list what you would miss if you did not achieve this goal.

You are now at the point of choice. You decide: Do I concentrate on the positive or negative?

SECTION THREE

Everyone Needs a Mentor

"Without inspiration the best powers of the mind remain dormant, there is a fuel in us which needs to be ignited with sparks."

Johann Gottfried von Herder

German philosopher, theologian, poet, and literary critic

The First Time

I was scared. After all, I was just three years old. The long black tunnel seemed to go forever and had my father not been holding my hand, I probably would have been crying. Then all of a sudden, the sunlight burst through the dark, and this great majestic monument filled with the most beautiful green grass I had ever seen was right in front of me. This was *the first time* I saw Yankee Stadium.

The year was 1949. My father was a diehard Yankee fan. He had mentioned on more than one occasion about having been at Yankee Stadium for Lou Gehrig Day, Babe Ruth Day and numerous World Series. But this was going to be my very first trip to Yankee Stadium. For weeks before, he kept telling me how big it was, how green it was and how many times history had been made there.

At three years old, I could not really comprehend all this. In fact, my father had spoken of the Yankees with such reverence that I had begun to think that we might be going to the Wailing Wall in Israel! He had told me lots of stories about the greats: Joe DiMaggio, Lou Gehrig, Babe Ruth, and others. I knew all of them like they were my own family.

My mother was not a fan, but she *was* my father's biggest fan. As a result, she took me shopping for the finest Yankee uniform that a three-year-old could wear. We searched store after store and finally found the perfect one. On the back was a big numeral five, the number belonging to Joe DiMaggio, my father's favorite player. As the big day got closer, I got more and more excited about going with my father to see his favorite team in action.

On the morning of the game, my dad and I ate breakfast together. When it was time to get into uniform, my mom helped me. First, I put on my socks and those really long leggings that they used to wear.

They went up to my mid thigh. Then I slipped on the pants, which were 100-percent wool. Then I put my arms into the shirt, which was also made of wool. A baseball cap completed the outfit. If you think that Joe DiMaggio looked great in his uniform, you should have seen me! Of course, I took my glove along just in case I caught a fly ball. (To this day, I've never caught a ball at a game!)

The excitement was palpable as my father gave me a pep talk: "Come on, Yankee. Let's go to the game." We jumped into the car and drove from Kew Garden Hills (where the only grass I had ever seen was the three feet surrounding each tree with yards of concrete in between) to Yankee Stadium in the Bronx. The trip took approximately one hour. However, I thought we were going to California or someplace like that because I had never been in the car for that long! As we crossed over the bridge to the Bronx, my dad kept telling me about all the famous Yankees that we would be able to see today. You can imagine how pleased I was at the prospect of seeing all these famous players in one place.

Finally, there it was, right in front of me: The huge concrete façade of Yankee Stadium! I was excited beyond my wildest dreams. It seemed like it took forever to park the car. My dad took my hand, and we walked towards this majestic looking place. Just picture me in full Yankee regalia, holding my daddy's hand, in total awe of the situation. As we got closer to the stadium, it loomed even larger. I didn't think that my neck could look that high up! My dad opened the door and in front of me I saw the Great Hall. Pictures of all of my favorite Yankees hung like huge flags. I really don't remember walking because it was more like floating. As we passed one after the other after the other, I got more and more excited. Looking up at my father (my idol) and all the Yankees was really too much for me to comprehend. It seemed too good to be true!

We stopped and picked up a program for twenty-five cents. Now I had pictures of the Yankees that I could hold in my hands. Unbelievable! We walked and walked through very narrow concrete hallways filled with lots of people. As I clutched my father's hand as hard as I could, we finally entered the long dark scary hallway I referred to earlier. As we walked to the light, I was both scared and excited. As we reached the end of the tunnel, all I saw was green. The grass was manicured so beautifully and the diamond cut so precisely that I figured we must be in heaven!

We found our seats and sat down. The guy behind us voiced his approval of me: "You've got the right uniform and number on!" My dad just smiled. As the lineups were announced, my dad told me about each one of the players. I don't really remember the team the Yankees played, which team won, or what the score was. However, I do remember thinking that I was with my favorite person in the perfect environment. Up to that point, it was the greatest day in my life (and in some respects, still is).

Over the years, I have often relived this day. I believe that each of us needs to play these kinds of fond memories over and over again in the mind. After all, it's not the negative aspects of your life that keep you going; it's the positive reinforcement of good things and good outcomes that is important to your well-being.

Let's fast-forward to the day when I took my little boy to his first Yankee game. We did the very same things that I had done with my father. Like my father and I, both of us just brimmed with absolute excitement, joy, happiness and love! At one point, I looked at him and said: "I promise you that you'll remember this day when you take your child to his or her first Yankee game."

Life sometimes throws you curves from which you think you may never recuperate. You may experience the death of someone close to you, an unfortunate incident in your life, a health problem, or other things of a negative nature. But, remember, the more you concentrate on the good things that have happened to you along the way, the more you might be able to defray or even remove the negative effect of what might be troubling you. Life is based on choices where you can take one path or another. Based on your experience, knowledge and expertise, you can make a choice that can help bring you out of your particular problem or deeper into it.

As the father of positive thinking, Earl Nightingale, once said: "It is the presence of your currently dominant thought which will dictate where you go." In other words, whether you think you can or can't, you're correct!

Things to Think About

Go through your memory bank, and pick out an occasion when you can remember feeling really good. It may be your first ballgame, a milestone birthday, your wedding day, or some other event that really pleased you.

- Now get into the scene. Try and duplicate those warm, fuzzy feelings that you experienced back then. Make that picture bigger, brighter, and bring it closer to you. At the height of your imagining the scene, touch your thumb and first finger together. Now open your eyes. Repeat this procedure three times, making sure to touch your thumb and first finger at the height of your imagined scene.
- After completing this exercise, the next time that you touch your thumb and first finger together, you will reproduce that warm, fuzzy feeling. On the other hand, if you do the same exercise with a negative picture in mind, you can also successfully reproduce those negative results!
- I often perform this exercise using the moment that I described in the previous story: I am three years old, with my father at my side, and I view Yankee Stadium for the first time. It makes me feel so good!

What could make you feel better?

School Days

I think most people would agree that going to college requires an adjustment to major changes in their life. For me, it was even more difficult because I was an only child and had relied so much on my mother, especially to help me with my schoolwork. After performing the research for a high-school assignment, I would lie down on the couch and dictate to my mother, who would translate my thoughts into English and grammar that people could more readily understand. After all, my mother had been a writer on The New York Times for many years, so her ability to create a good story was unmatched. I never really wrote anything by myself!

With much trepidation, I went off to college. Apparently, this was different from high school where things were handed to you. Not only were you expected to do all the research, but also, to actually write the paper. This was totally new!

Thank goodness, I had chosen to major in biology. However, in a liberal arts school, you must undertake a smattering of all of the disciplines. Therefore, I also had requirements in a foreign language (yuck), math (double yuck), history, and my favorite subject of all, English! (I liked the latter about as much as I liked walking on broken glass!)

Toward the end of the semester, my English teacher announced that a paper was due for our final examination. Total shock went through my body! Nonetheless, I managed to do the research because that was fun, but then I attempted to write the paper. I must have spent two or three days trying to put this research paper together. Considering my shortcomings, I thought I had done a relatively good job. At the end of this project, I asked my roommate—an English major—to critique my work. Since he was a nice guy and concerned about hurting my feelings, he told me the paper was okay. However, he did show me some areas where I could improve it. So, I rewrote the paper, changing what he had told me to change. Then, I asked him read it again. He said that the revisions were good, and the paper was okay to submit.

Having taken into account my roommate's criticisms and his corrections, I thought I had handed in a good paper— not a masterpiece—but still a good paper. Approximately three days later, my English professor called me into the English faculty room. Imagine my surprise when he asked me was if I was a functional illiterate! With a stunned look on my face, I asked him what he meant. He said that a few people are admitted each year that don't have the true intellect for college, but they are admitted to fill quota numbers. Apparently, he was referring to me! I told him that to the best of my knowledge, I had an IQ in triple digits and that I thought of myself as a fairly intelligent person. He thought that was *hysterical!* After his laughter settled down, he told me in no uncertain terms that this was the worst term paper that he had ever seen in his entire teaching career. Furthermore, he said that I would need a miracle to pass his class!

To add insult to injury, the entire English department had been privy to his statement about my being a functional illiterate, as well as my answer to him. They in turn were laughing hysterically. When I explained that, although I couldn't write well, I was a scientist and did things in a very logical and succinct manner, their laughter reached a roar!

By my senior year, my writing skills had improved significantly. In fact, I was selected by my mentor to write a scientific paper on the DNA code of a particular strain of E. Coli. I accomplished the challenging task with little trouble. By then, I had learned that this was not high school and you really needed to put the work into college to get what you wanted out of it.

Because I majored in biology, I had been assigned a counselor in the biology department: Dr. Richard Segina. During the three years that he counseled me, I gained more self-confidence and did very well. Another of my professors was Dr. Carol Bocher. She taught me as much about life as she did about biology. I cannot thank her enough for her input, support, and guidance. These two professors epitomized what education should be! The function of a teacher is to educate and inspire. These professors excelled at both!

You can imagine where my head was after my encounter with the English professor. I didn't know if I could make it, what major I would pursue, or what I was going to do for a living. I didn't know how I was going to deal with making decisions that would affect the rest of my life.

These two wonderful people each sat down with me at different times and counseled me on how to be a good person. Neither one of them dealt a lot with the academic side of my life, but they both paid close attention to how I was dealing psychologically with school and being away from home. I spent many hours talking to them. Over time, I was able to forge my life in a constructive and positive way. As you try to find your way, you need people who are more interested in helping you than they are in stroking their own egos. People such as Dr. Segina and Dr. Bocher exemplify this philosophy. They taught me how to take large amounts of material and prioritize them into a plan of action.

When I was a chiropractic student, I was approached by an underclassman who told me that he had decided to quit school. He explained that not only was he working full-time, but he also had responsibilities as a husband, father, and homeowner. He just couldn't imagine how he would be able to do it all.

I sat with him over a cup of coffee and began to listen to his problems. After about ten minutes, he asked me if I had any suggestions. I told him that I was also working a full-time job and going to school full-time; and that I had a wife, two children, and a mortgage. I was just like him. I asked him what he would gain by being a chiropractor and what he would lose if he were unable to accomplish this goal for his life. He thanked me for my time and left.

About a month later, I was summoned to the president's office. You can imagine the amount of consternation that went through my mind being called to the president's office.

Dr. Napolitano was a giant in the chiropractic profession. He was tall, with a booming voice and incredibly intelligent. The secretary let me into his office and told me to sit down. Dr. Napolitano came up to me, shook my hand, and told me that I would be a great chiropractor because I was developing into a truly caring human being.

Dr. Napolitano explained that he had received a letter from a student. The student wrote that I had taken the time and effort to sit down with him, listen to him, and give good advice as to his future. The student was so taken with my openness and willingness to listen that he had decided to stay in school based on our conversation. Then, the president asked me to become a member of his President's Council because of my ability to help people!

During my years as a college professor, I was always open to students who wanted to talk about academics or anything else for that matter. In addition to being a resource person, I became a sounding board for the students. I have found that these kinds of opportunities that allow you to truly help someone are also opportunities that can make you a better person.

Often, all it takes to help people is to listen. Just be receptive to them and hear their story with an open mind. If you have something positive to contribute, be willing to share it. Try this next time someone comes to you in need. You would be surprised how simple and effective listening can be.

You can also use this technique as a negotiating tool for yourself. Be open to your thoughts, don't judge yourself, and seek advice when you are confused. If you can change the negative thinking to positive thinking, just watch where you will go!

Things to Think About

Who do you look up to? What about this person makes them so special?

- Make a list of this person's positive attributes.

Now look at yourself. Are you a person that other people look up to?

- List all of your positive attributes.

Now, strive to be the best you can be!

The Mick

It was 1956. My father and I were going together to a Yankee game. Talk about excitement! I'm going with my live-in idol to see another one of my idols, who was larger than life: Mickey Mantle! I can recall it like it was yesterday. How could I forget that huge majestic form of a man with a big number seven on his back? From my seat down on the first base side, I could see his forearm muscles rippling with each grip of his mighty bat. The pitch headed toward him and that prodigious swing propelled the baseball over 350 feet into the right-field bleachers. It was just another home run from my idol! Of course, the Yankees won the game.

What is a mentor? Is it someone who inspires you? Is it someone who pushes you or is it someone who tells you that you can be better than you think you are? In my opinion, it is a person who demonstrates qualities you would like to emulate. I can remember trying to run like Mickey Mantle, talk with a southern drawl like Mickey Mantle, and basically do everything the way I thought Mickey Mantle did. At ten-years-old, I really had no idea what kind of man that Mickey Mantle really was, but I sure knew what kind of a baseball player he was!

As I grew up, I learned that Mickey Mantle, as a real person, was as flawed as any other human being. My generation discovered that Mickey was a drinker and loved the nightlife. Had my father known the whole truth, I am sure that he would not have approved of me emulating the lifestyle of Mickey Mantle.

As the sports memorabilia business became popular, so did Mickey Mantle's resurgence into the limelight. He was asked to appear at countless baseball signings. In fact, his signature was one of the most sought-after autographs. People even named their children after Mickey. The Mick surely did not understand how influential he really was!

When baseball lovers found out that Mickey Mantle needed a liver transplant or he would die, they were shocked. But Mickey was big enough to admit that he had made mistakes. In fact, after he got that transplant, he went from a drunken has-been baseball player to a real hero. He told the world that he had treated his body poorly and had to pay the price for it. He urged people to use him as an example of what not to do. In one fell swoop, he may have changed the lives of millions of people. He became a beacon for a healthy lifestyle and a spokesman for organ donation. Even though he did not live a long period of time after his transplant, Mickey's message of being responsible for your own health will live as long as his contribution to baseball.

You, too, may be a mentor to a many of different people. Remember, people are watching you and observing you. They see not only what you do, but also how you go about doing it. Do you do tasks willingly or do you consider it a chore? Do you volunteer to help people even though it would not benefit you in any way? Do you ask yourself what can I do today to make other people happy or better? The function of life is to improve yourself on a daily basis. If you looked back on your life, would you say that you helped people along the way or did you step over them to get what you want?

In my personal experience, I have had the great fortune of having many different mentors. Several were teachers, others were clergy, and yes, a few were sports figures. From each of these people, I took away pearls of wisdom that enriched my life and enabled me to enrich the lives of others. You don't have to be wealthy or hold a high position to be a mentor.

Things to Think About

Sit down and compile a list of mentors in your life.

- For the purpose of this exercise, exclude family members.
- Once you have compiled this list, take a moment to thank each of these people for the gifts that they have given you.
- Now the tough part. Think of how you have used the teachings of your mentors to help other people. If your mentors could critique your efforts, would they be pleased? If so, keep on doing what you are doing. If you don't think they would be pleased, what changes could you make to have them smile down with you and say: "Good job!"

Remember, it's your choice. Choose carefully!

SECTION FOUR

Faith

"You miss 100 percent of the shots you don't take."

Wayne Gretzky
Famous International Ice Hockey Star

Just Love

"How will I recognize you?" I asked the woman, a stranger on the other end of the phone. She said: "I have blonde hair and big arms." I thought I was going to meet a Russian wrestler! Instead, I met the love of my life.

After twenty-eight years of marriage, my ex-wife and I had decided it was time to end our relationship. Many people stay married until it becomes just too uncomfortable to live with each other. Despite the inevitable conclusion, the separation process is very painful, and in my case, very ugly. It seems that divorce really brings out the worst in people. Enough said about that!

The good news was that I was single again. I was finally free to do all of the great things that my failing marriage had prevented me from doing. I surveyed my physical situation. I was fifty-years-old with a full head of hair. Good news! I still had a flat stomach and was in relatively good physical condition. More good news! I am good-looking, and I am a physician. Very good news! I have an outgoing personality and enjoy people. The best news!

On the outside, the situation looked great. Unfortunately, that was just the front page. When you turned the page to read the rest of whole story, the outcome was less attractive. Mentally, I was in a really bad state. Let's face it: When you are depressed, nothing seems right. So there I was, going on date after date, and becoming more and more discouraged.

As an anal-retentive person, I decided to make a goal sheet with the qualities that my prospective love would possess. I listed such things as height, weight, age, physical condition, religion, personality, interests, likes, and dislikes. I made these goals as specific as possible in order to create my ideal mate. Finally, I decided on ten specific criteria for this ideal mate. I read these in front of a mirror in the morning and at night. In addition, I thought about them constantly throughout the day. I visualized this magnificent human being, someday, dropping into my life!

Date after date came and went. I must have met the strangest, most neurotic people in the world! Now, I know that my negative mental attitude attracted these people into my life. For example, I was on a date with an attractive female who asked me how many years I was married. I told her that I had been married for twenty-eight years. She looked at me and said: "There must be something wrong with you! You can you take me home now."

There were others that were just as bizarre. After one year of reading my goals several times a day, I just wasn't feeling any emotion anymore. So, I decided to just read them once a day. Once you have a plan, the most important part of reaching your goal may be just "letting go and letting it happen." If you press and concentrate too hard, you can push the goal or ideal situation further away from you.

About two months later, I was working out in the gym and a young lady came up to me. She got right to the point: "Are you the doctor that's getting divorced?" With all of the testosterone that I could muster, I replied: "I certainly am." She said: "Have I got a girl for you!" Now, in my book, that means that the girl is tainted in *some way!* If the young lady at the gym had added, "and she has a great personality," I would have never given her my card. But, I did give her my card, and she promised to pass it on.

During office hours the next day, my beeper went off. I usually take care of calls during my break. So, when my break came, I called back the number on the beeper. The person who answered on the other end said: "You have the wrong number." I hung up and tried the number again. In a nasty voice, the same woman on the other end of the phone answered: "I said you have the wrong number." Then, she hung up on me again. To say the least, I was confused. But honestly, I quickly forgot about the incident.

The next day my beeper went off again. Something told me to call this person back, despite the fear of verbal repercussions. Instead of the nasty woman, I reached a very lovely sounding person on the phone. We talked for period of time. In all honesty, I still had no idea who she was. She finally said that her nail lady gave her my card. We made arrangements to meet that Friday night. She had mentioned that she loved to dance, so we were going to meet at a dance club after my Friday night commitments.

It was winter, so I wore a wool herringbone jacket with a sweater turtleneck. When we had talked on the phone, I had asked her how I would recognize her that Friday. That was when she had famously described herself: "I have blonde hair and *big arms*." As I mentioned before, I thought I was going to meet a Russian wrestler!

Friday night arrived, and I was on my way to the dance club to meet my Russian wrestler. When I got there, I looked around, only to discover that there were many blonde-haired women. I tried to picture her image in my head, a blonde with big arms. All of a sudden, I saw her! Rather than big, I saw her arms as beautiful well-sculptured appendages attached to an attractive torso. In other words, she was a beautiful specimen of womanhood!

We proceeded to go upstairs to the dance club. After about ten minutes of dancing while wearing a herringbone jacket, I figured it was time for me to strip. Off came the jacket, but the perspiration continued! We danced for three full hours, and it was the best three hours I had spent in a very long time. We left the dance club together, and I walked her back to her car. We promised each other that we would talk again soon. Then, we kissed. Just once! However, there was something special about this kiss.

About one week later, we made arrangements to meet. It was a last-minute thing, so we really had not planned where to go. To make matters worse, it was Halloween, and parties were going on all over.

We managed to find a small tavern where we could sit at a table, have some wine, and just talk. Unfortunately, we were approximately twenty to thirty years younger than anyone else in the establishment! But, we really didn't care. We talked for hours and found that we had a lot in common.

We made arrangements to see each other again, and I am happy to say that we are still seeing each other! So, you might ask, what about the goals that I had been determined to reach when I set them fourteen months before? This woman fulfilled nine of the ten criteria that I had written down. The only goal that had not been fulfilled was that she was not a multimillionaire.

I learned a lot from my divorce. I had to get straight in my head what was most important for me, and then execute that plan. One part of the plan was to find a woman who was compatible with me. After setting up specific criteria for each one of my goals, I needed to believe that these goals would actually come true.

Remaining confident that you will eventually succeed may be the most difficult part of striving to reach a goal. Most people do not give themselves enough pats on the back. They will cut themselves down quickly, but be slow to ever give themselves a compliment.

My biggest doubt was that I would actually find someone who would fit the criteria. I had lost faith, but I just did what I was taught, and then, I eventually let go. In the letting go, I allowed the universe to vibrate in concert with me. In other words, I negotiated with myself to be satisfied with what I had been given. In return, I received the absolute love of my life: Corinne!

Things to Think About

Write down a positive statement about something you want.

- Read the statement three times per day for seven days while looking in the mirror.
- Then, read the statement two times a day for another seven days while looking in the mirror.
- Finally, read the statement one time per day for seven more days while looking in the mirror.

At the end of these three weeks, you should be able to repeat that statement as if it were fact. In truth, it will be. You have just consciously created a habit. Congratulations!

Parachute

Here I am, sitting cross-legged in the fuselage of a plane and about to jump out at 14,000 feet. What did I get myself into? Did I have a death wish? Although I had already walked on hot coals to prove to myself that the mind is more powerful than the body, somehow jumping out of a perfectly good airplane seemed a little too much!

The whole thing had started a few months before during the summer of 1988, when I was associated with a group of people studying neurolinguistic programming. One of the principles is to challenge oneself beyond what you thought was possible. I was in my early forties and eager to test myself.

The first step was to spend a day investigating your ability to focus. At the end of the day, the challenge was to walk across hot coals for approximately twelve feet. If the technique worked, you would not feel any pain because you had directed your mind elsewhere. I really did do that and did not burn my feet. So I had met the first challenge.

However, I have always been a person who investigates things to the nth degree. The second challenge was to skydive. Beginning skydivers can jump by going tandem or solo. In a tandem skydive, you are attached to a jumpmaster, and he does the skydiving. The other method requires you to jump out of the plane by yourself. Then you are met in midair by two jumpmasters who direct your descent.

In order to jump out of the plane by yourself or solo, you are required to attend six hours of school. You learn the correct position to descend. You also rehearse over and over how to pull your parachute and how to direct it after it opens. Experienced skydivers pack their own chutes, but first-timers like me have them packed for us.

Although still on the ground, you get into a harness so you can practice how to direct the descent of the parachute. The instructor tells you to dislodge the toggles from the Velcro that attaches them to the chute, and then pull the toggle in a particular direction. You are further taught to pull the toggles in sequence so that your descent is more controlled. The instructor told us to pull both toggles down hard when you are approximately twenty feet off the deck. To make things easier, an instructor would be on the ground with a headset directing you. The course also covered landing techniques.

The six hours were up and we were ready for our first jump. However the weather did not cooperate, so we were sent home and expected back in the morning. That night I called my wife (now ex-wife). I told her what I was about to do. Her only response to me was: "Have you paid your life insurance?" I said yes, and she said goodbye. That night—instead of sleeping—I was practicing how to fall through the air at approximately 131 miles per hour. I practiced the proper placement of my hands when pulling the ripcord. I went over and over in my head how to pull the toggles and direct my descent to the ground.

Despite the practice, I was not calm when I got up the next morning. In fact, I felt quite nervous. We took the shuttle and arrived at the skydive airstrip to continue with our training, with the goal of jumping out of that perfectly good airplane.

The flight instructors went over exactly how to exit the aircraft while it is going approximately eighty miles an hour at 14,000 feet. They directed us to make "an aggressive step out," and then place one foot on the very small step and your hands on the under portion of the wing. After that you were to: "Just let go!" After you had "just let go," two jumpmasters would follow you and hold on to your harness directing you until you pulled the ripcord. If you should somehow forget to pull the ripcord, they will do that for you (nice of them)!

We then proceeded to the aircraft to practice getting in and out of the plane and how to properly stand while jumping. Since the airplane was still on the ground, we all did that with no problem.

Then it was back to the hangar to put on our jumpsuits. As I was putting on my jumpsuit, a male instructor approached me. He told me that before I put on the jumpsuit, I needed to make sure that I pull down my fly and rearrange the contents within. Responding, I said I really didn't like him that much! We both laughed and proceeded to the airplane.

Skydiving assignments were handed out. My jumpmasters were actually a couple. In fact, the guy happened to be the one who advised me about my jumpsuit situation. He was married to a very good-looking woman. We proceeded to the plane. The female jumpmaster had gotten in first and sat in the back facing me. I then got into the plane. Since the plane was really small, the only way I could fit was to straddle my legs around the female jumpmaster. This made me really uncomfortable because all I could think of was this guy getting mad at me and not helping me pull my shoot! I started to sweat profusely.

The propeller started and the plane began to move. Picture this, I have my hands crossed in front of my chest, my legs are straddled around this female instructor, and I'm sweating like it's 800 degrees Fahrenheit. The airplane started to circle up and up and up. As we got close to 14,000 feet, the male instructor opened the hatch. The rush of air almost caused me to pass out, but I tried to remain as calm as possible. I placed my goggles over my eyes and gave him a thumbs-up. Then I made "an aggressive step out" onto this teeny, tiny step 14,000 feet above the earth, while placing my hands on the underside of the wing. I then "just let go!"

I could not believe that I was falling through the air. Suddenly, all the training went out the window, too, and I started to flail my arms and legs like crazy. Thankfully, the two jumpmasters were able to guide me so that I became fairly stable. However, I was sweating so much that my goggles started to fog. In desperation, I placed both hands on the goggles and lifted them, expelling the water. With my sight restored, I was able to look at my altimeter and saw it was time to pull the ripcord. I signaled to the jumpmasters, and they both gave me the thumbs-up, so I pulled the cord.

During our training, the instructors had told us that within fifty feet after pulling the rip cord, you go from descending 131 miles per hour to zero miles per hour! Therefore, you will feel a "slight tug" between your legs. (Remember the male flight instructor and his zipper proposal?) To be honest, that did not come to mind as I was pulling the ripcord because I was so intent on doing it right. When I did pull the ripcord, that "slight tug" they had talked about was in reality the ultimate wedgy! After the discomfort subsided, the ride was great.

Now I had to get control of the toggles. When I had practiced this before, we were on the ground, and it was easy to get the toggles because I was on my tiptoes. However, getting on your tiptoes is useless at 5,000 feet in the air. The only way I could possibly reach the toggles was to purposefully sway the parachute side to side, so I did. The guy with the headpiece on the ground screamed at me to get control of the parachute. No kidding! At last, I was able to get a hold of one toggle, and then the other. A voice blared in my ear "turn left," so I pulled on the left toggle. He bellowed again: "I said turn left!" So, I pulled on the toggle some more. By now, he is screaming: "Turn left! Turn left!" Finally, I figured out that he was looking at me so his left was really my right. So I pulled on the right toggle, and he screamed with relief: "That's better!" There I was 5,000 feet in the air with my parachute open, and I appeared dyslexic. When he said right, I pulled left!

Now it was time to land. Remember, he was supposed to tell me to pull both toggles. I'm listening for the signal and suddenly he screams: "Pull both toggles!" So I do, and I bend my knees with my two feet together expecting to land on my feet. The truth of the matter is that my rear hit before anything, and I slid approximately twenty feet. It didn't even resemble the landing of anyone on the Golden Knights of the Army parachute team.

Well, there it is, my experience skydiving. I think this episode is a classic example of negotiating with myself. First of all, I had to weigh the pros and cons of doing the actual skydive. Then, I had to make a choice between doing it tandem or solo. Then, I had to rehearse the position to skydive enough times to create muscle memory. I had to rehearse pulling the toggles and how to land. All of these steps required that I make choices. The more information you gather, the better your decisions.

If I overcame the challenges of walking on hot coals and skydiving, I believe that anyone can overcome their limitations and accomplish things that they thought they never would. Go for your dreams! You might just achieve them!

Things to Think About

Here is a fun game for you to play. You need two people to play this game.

- Stand up straight, and hold your hands out in front of you palms together. Now, as carefully as you can, rotate your body from one side to the other. Have the other person mark where your limits of twisting end.
- Now, close your eyes, and repeat the procedure with the thought that you can twist further. Have the person mark your progress this time. Usually you will find that you are able to twist further with your eyes closed because you have eliminated the limiting factor (your eyes).

This is a fun way to prove that you can do more than you think you can, if you:
"Just let go!"

Where Is the Pony?

There once were two identical twins: One was named Harry, and the other was named Barry. As they grew up, they developed marked differences in their personalities. Harry was an extremely introverted, anti-social, and anxious child. On the other hand, Barry was a gregarious, outgoing, and fun-loving kid.

The situation perplexed their parents to the point that they sought psychological care for Harry and Barry. The parents were referred to an optimist/pessimist specialist. The children were ushered into the doctor's office and interviewed extensively by him. The psychologist decided that he needed to keep the children for a week in order to observe their behavior.

First, the psychologist placed Harry in a room with all the perks of Disney World. Every conceivable toy, game, ride, or food item was available to the boy. He told Harry to have a good time, and he would see him soon. Then, the psychologist closed the door and walked away. On the other hand, the psychologist put the other twin, Barry, in a room that was more like a stable. It smelled to high heaven with piles of horse manure! He informed Barry that he was going to stay there for a week.

The week went by, and the parents were eager to find out exactly how each of their children had fared. Accompanied by the doctor, they anxiously opened the door of Harry's room, only to see Harry in the corner of this wonderful room crying his eyes out. They walked over to Harry and asked him what was wrong. Harry told him that he didn't know what to do with himself for the entire week. They asked him if he tried any of the rides, and he said no because he was afraid he would throw up. They asked him if he ate some of the delicious food, and he said that he ate very little because he was afraid he was going to get sick. Then they asked him if he enjoyed any of the toys and games, and Harry said that he didn't want to play because he was afraid that he might hurt himself.

With desperation in their eyes, the parents looked at the psychologist and asked: "What can we do for this child?" The psychologist replied: "I am not sure if there is anything we can do. I am afraid that Harry is a hopeless pessimist."

Fearing more bad news, they walked into Barry's room. To their surprise, they saw Barry playing contently. In fact, he was laughing while having the time of his life digging through the mounds of horse manure. The parents went up to Barry and asked him: "Why are you are so happy?" Optimist that he was, Barry replied: "Underneath all this manure has to be a pony!"

What you think about the most is probably what you're going to get. Let's take a look at Harry's attitude: It sucked! No matter what anybody said or did, his response was always negative. Remember, *like attracts like,* so the more Harry thought about what was going to go wrong, the more *went* wrong. On the other hand, Barry's attitude was always positive. Although faced with many obstacles, Barry kept his eye on the prize and envisioned a pony at the end of his digging. Even though he never found the pony, his attitude was still great. This is called faith. Without faith, there is no belief, and remember that *belief drives the engine.*

Although Harry and Barry were identical twins, each had totally different views of the world. One saw the glass half-full and the other, half-empty. Which one of the twins are you like? Do you look for the good in situations or are you constantly complaining, blaming others, and rationalizing why you're in a less-than-optimal situation? The more you believe in a positive outcome, the more positive outcomes will come to you.

Things to Think About

Pick a subject about which you feel slightly negative.

- Why do you feel negative about this particular situation?
- Sit down in a quiet place and visualize the situation.
- In your mind's eye, take the negative situation and change it to a positive outcome.

Here's a hint: Changing the way you look, hear, touch, taste, and smell about the visualized image can help you achieve the preferred outcome.

SECTION FIVE

Experience

"We are what we repeatedly do. Excellence, therefore, is not an act but a habit."

Aristotle
Greek Philosopher

My First Workout

When entering into your chosen occupation, you should look and feel the part. As a health professional, one needs to present themselves in good physical condition. After all, it would be difficult for you to tell one of your patients to lose weight if you were forty or fifty pounds overweight yourself. That wouldn't make sense to them.

Throughout chiropractic college, the professors impressed upon us that physical conditioning is very important in both presentation to the patient and your longevity as a practitioner. The better shape you are in physically, the more confidently you can tell people to lose weight if that is one of their major problems. Furthermore, it is important to be in good physical condition because of the physical demands required of you when adjusting large numbers of people.

After completing my chiropractic education, I decided to take heed and make sure that I was in the best physical shape possible. The easiest way to do this was to join a gym. I found a gym near my office and visited there to inquire about how to start a personal physical fitness program. This was the late seventies and early eighties when progressive resistance training was in its infancy and little was known about the long-term effects.

Health clubs made their money by taking people through incredibly long and difficult weightlifting routines, counting on the fact that they would be so sore the next day that they would quit and not come back. As I was unfamiliar with this practice, I walked into the health club and asked to meet with the proprietor. He was a massive individual who exclaimed that I had a great frame to build on. I suspected he was just stroking my ego, but the encouragement made me much more amenable to joining.

After signing up, I went into the locker room and changed. He took me through this incredibly intense, weighty, and difficult routine. The session was over in approximately one hour. Afterward, I felt a little bit nauseous and extremely tired. To top off the day, I had office hours in the afternoon.

I showered, changed, and proceeded to go to the office. As I was driving, I realized that my arms were a little bit shaky and my whole body was extremely tired. I walked into my office, saw that the reception room was filled with patients, and started my afternoon hours.

The first patient I treated that day was a very thin young lady who told me she had mid-back problems. I asked her to get on the chiropractic table, face down, and proceeded with my analysis as to what segments of her spine I was planning to adjust. With that in mind, I proceeded to adjust her mid-back. I did not realize that my arms were very weak from the vigorous workout that I had endured just a little more than one hour prior to this. As I tried to adjust her, my arms collapsed, my head dropped, and my face dove onto her mid-back.

To say the least, she was shocked about what just happened. Quite honestly, so was I! She turned her head, looked at me and said: "Doctor: Is this a new type of technique?" I responded: "Yes, this is the nasium technique. The purpose of it is to smell where the subluxations are." For whatever reason, she was satisfied with that explanation. I finished adjusting her and sent her on her way.

The rest of the afternoon was difficult for me, because I had no real strength to be able to properly adjust the quantity of people that had been scheduled. Nonetheless, I was able to finish my office hours and went home. That evening, I made sure to take a hot shower and go right to bed. As I awoke the next morning, I realized that the only places that did not hurt were my eyes. This soreness lasted a few days. However, I stuck with it and have been doing progressive resistance training for the past thirty-five years!

This story is an example of the potential consequences of dealing with the unknown. Had I known the amount of soreness that I would go through after the first workout, I might have been able to reschedule that appointment so that it would not interfere with my practice. You see, the more information that you receive before you make a decision, the more competent the decision will be and the outcomes are likely to be more beneficial to all involved.

Things to Think About

How do you make decisions? One should make decisions based on knowledge, experience and desire.

- Pick a situation and write down all of the possible outcomes that could happen.
- Now list them in a format by putting the most pressing matter first.

In order for you to put all these outcomes in order of importance, you have to make choices. This is the art of internal negotiation. If you finished the exercise, you just practiced that art!

Same Old Way, Same Old Results

A long time ago, in a far-off land, lived a man who asked: "How do I become rich beyond my wildest dreams?" A friend suggested that he seek the advice of the wisest man in the entire kingdom. When the man found him, the wise man told him of the legend of the touchstone.

The touchstone was said to be so powerful that the man who found it would gain all the knowledge he needed to attain tremendous wealth. The unique characteristic of this touchstone was its temperature. It is warm to the touch. Moreover, this touchstone could only be found in the Dead Sea!

Excited by this information, the man sold all his valuables and set out on the journey to find the touchstone. He was confident that if he could just hold this touchstone in his hand, he would become the richest man in the world.

The man finally reached the Dead Sea. Besides the water, he could see nothing but stones and more stones—hundreds and millions of stones! How was he to find the touchstone in all of these stones? Then he remembered what the wisest man in the kingdom had told him. He had said that the touchstone was warm to the touch, while all other stones were cold to the touch. So, one by one, he would pick up each stone and feel it. If the stone was cold, he would throw it back to the sea. Eventually, he would discover the warm stone, which would be the answer to all his troubles.

On the first day, the man enthusiastically picked up the first stone. However, it was cold, so he threw it back into the sea. Then he picked up another stone, which was also cold, so he threw that back into the sea. For the rest of the day, then a whole week, and then a whole month, he picked up stones. Each and every one of them was cold, so he threw them back into the sea.

This went on for months. During this time, the man grew tired and discouraged. Nonetheless, he was determined and tried to keep up his enthusiasm so he could reach his goal. He continued to pick up stones one at a time. If the stone was cold, he threw it back into the sea.

A year had passed, but he vowed to keep looking for the touchstone. Day after day, he got up in the morning and went to work as enthusiastically as still possible to find the touchstone. Over and over, he would pick up a stone, feel it cold to the touch, and throw it into the sea.

After two years, the man was still poor, plus sick and tired. By now, he was just working by rote with no thought or enthusiasm behind it. He picked up a stone, but it was cold, so he threw it back into the sea. He picked up another stone; *it was warm*, yet he still threw it back into the sea!

The moral to the story is if you do the same old thing, in the same old way, you will get the same old results! Behave in a different way and guess what, you might (just might) get a different result.

To illustrate the positive aspect of this phenomenon, consider a true story of persistence with enthusiasm. As a cantor, I perform wedding ceremonies as one of my functions. When constructing a ceremony, I find that it's important to find out the background of the bride and bridegroom. In our modern day, approximately twenty percent of all marriages come about through use of a dating service. On one occasion, a bride told me that she had gone on over ninety first-dates before she found the person with whom she fell in love.

The bride said she had approached each date with enthusiasm and an air of positive expectation. After each unsuccessful date, she reevaluated her priorities and set out to move in a different direction. In other words, she did not repeat her mistakes. She had a clear mental picture of the kind of man she wanted. Then, she just enjoyed the process of searching for him. I was touched when she told me: "My future husband is exactly who God wanted me to have."

As we try to make goals, we need to fuel each goal with enthusiasm. If you don't have some fuel behind your drive, you are driving in neutral or reverse! Once you learn what does not work, why would you try and do it again the same way? By the way, this is the definition of insanity: doing the same thing in the same way and expecting a different result!

The first thing to do is to state your goal. What do you truly want? You can't get what you want if you don't know what you want. Once you know what you want, go get it! Formulate a plan of action, and then execute the action with thought and enthusiasm. The most difficult part of the process is to keep your spirits up while keeping your eye on the goal. Each day is a new day. Wake up with enthusiasm, and get going!

Things to Think About

Would you like to change something about yourself?

- Make a list of all of the characteristics that you want to change. List all the things that you do presently, and then list the changes that you want to occur.
- Now focus on one of the changes and concentrate on doing that for one week.
- At the end of the week, take an inventory as to how the change affected your total behavior process. If the outcome was positive, keep the change and go on to the next one on your list. If there was no change or a negative change, you need to reevaluate the list.

It really is as simple as that. It just takes determination on your part and confidence in the knowledge that you are making yourself a better person.

Come On Man!

It had been a really long day. As I sat there behind my beautiful new desk, I contemplated the events that had taken place. I continued to shake my head and say: "Come on man! Are you kidding me?"

After four years of going to school full-time and working two full-time jobs, the goal was in sight. I had actually done it: All my life I had wanted to become a doctor! Now, behind my expensive desk in my beautiful new office, I was sitting in a chair that was much too big for my body. Nonetheless, I felt a sense of real accomplishment.

The day was filled with the arrival of new furniture, setting up each one of the rooms, then decorating the rooms and making them comfortable spaces for people to be treated. I had bought the newest in professional tables. They moved any-which way you could think of and were perfect for chiropractic work. All that was missing were patients!

Out of the blue, the telephone rang and somebody on the other end said: "I have bad, low-back pain. Can I come in and see you?" Looking up to the sky, I silently mouthed: "Thank you," and said to her: "Let me see if I have an opening." I waited to a full count of ten before I came back and replied: "I can see you in two hours. Is that okay?" She said: "I'll be there."

I hurried around the office making sure that everything was just perfect. I was eagerly awaiting my first experience in treating a real patient, not from the clinic as a mere intern, but, here in my own office, a real patient would be seen by a real doctor: *Me!* Boy, was I excited!

The moment arrived. In walks a woman bent over from pain with her boyfriend assisting her. As I told them which room to go into, I noticed that the gentleman was wearing a motorcycle jacket with "Hell's Angels" on the back. Well, I was no different from most people who are afraid of just the sight of that insignia. In addition, this was my *very first* real patient! So I paid extra special attention to take care of her so that this guy would not get upset in any way, shape, or form!

I gave the poor woman a very thorough physical examination (with him being present, of course). She had a condition that required me to adjust her in a way that might cause some discomfort. I informed her of exactly what I was going to do and told her that she might feel some discomfort initially, but that it would go away within a short period of time. I also told her to treat the area with moist heat, which would take care of most of that discomfort. She agreed to proceed. With fear and trepidation, I also looked at her boyfriend for silent assent. Then, I started the procedure.

The procedure went very well and I could tell by the end of the treatment that she would be just fine by tomorrow. However, when I adjusted her, she let out a little yell. In my experience, this is a very common occurrence. I really didn't think about it for a moment. I proceeded to bring the table to an upright position. As I turned to help the young lady off the table, the gentleman with the "Hell's Angels" jacket stuck the tip of a nine-inch hunting knife nearly into my stomach and said: "If you hurt her, I am going to cut you, you blankety-blank!"

It's amazing what goes through your head when you're faced with these types of situations. Here I had just spent the last four years of my life striving to make my life better for my family and me. Despite this, I could wind up dead after my first day of practice. What a concept!

Thank goodness, before I hit the real panic button, the young lady started to move side to side in a swaying motion and turned to her boyfriend and said, "No, Tommy. It feels real good. We can even have sex tonight." With that, he retracted the nine-inch hunting knife that seemed to be sticking into my belly and put it back into his boot. Then he gave me a check (which bounced), and they went on their way.

So you can truly say that my first day in practice was quite notable. As I had done shortly after the business day had begun, I ended the day looking up. Still grateful, this time I said: "Come on, man! You could've made it a little easier."

Things to Think About

Have you ever been thrown a real curve in your life; something that is out of the blue and is of real concern to you?

- How would you react?
- What would be your thinking process?
- What specific things would you do to come to a conclusion?
- List them and you will find that you have just gone through the process of self negotiation.

By repeating this procedure, you become more aware of the process and your ability to overcome obstacles.

SECTION SIX

Inspiration

"It is not the critic who counts: not the man who points out how the strong man stumbles or where the doer of deeds could have done better. The credit belongs to the man who is actually in the arena, whose face is marred by dust and sweat and blood, who strives valiantly, or errs and comes up short again and again, because there is no effort without error or shortcoming, but who knows the great enthusiasms, the great devotions, who spends himself for a worthy cause; who, at the best, knows, in the end, the triumph of high achievement and who, at the worst, if he fails, at the least he fails while daring greatly, so that his place shall never be with those cold and timid souls who knew neither victory nor defeat."

Theodore "Teddy" Roosevelt
Twenty-Sixth President of the United States

Row, Row, Row Your Boat

I was, angry, annoyed, and frustrated. Not only did I lose the award, but also my biggest competition won!

The Parker Seminar is the largest chiropractic seminar in the world. At the end of each year, the attendees vote for their choice of chiropractor of the year. For the past two years, I had been nominated for this honor and, unfortunately, did not win either time. Talk about an ego deflator! I had fought hard in my campaign for this award. I was ready with my acceptance speech, but, to my chagrin, the other guy got it. After the ceremony, with all the fake enthusiasm I could muster, I walked up and congratulated him on his achievement.

One of my best friends, who just happened to have been listening, approached me. He said: "You did the right thing by congratulating him." Then, he added: "Harris: Row, row, row your boat gently down the stream." I looked at him like he had six heads, and asked my friend what he was talking about! He explained that the best you can possibly do is travel down the river or stream, and try to avoid the obstacles. On the other hand, turning the boat upstream and fighting the current was not productive and actually detrimental. Wow! What great advice!

Think about it. From the time you are born till the time that you die, you are traveling down the river or stream of your life. Along the way, you encounter rapids, waterfalls, and even rocks that threaten to change your course. These represent the challenges in your life. One must try to navigate into the center of the river, and find the current that will take you down easiest. As you overcome each challenge, you gain experience and more knowledge. Should a similar set of circumstances present themselves again, you will be able to better navigate or negotiate the challenges (you now have more choices). With more choices, you are able to make more informed decisions.

As you navigate down the river of life, you can only see a little bit in front of you. You may not have a physical picture of your destination, but you must keep the image of this destination in your mind. Think of it as going on an airplane from New York to Los Angeles. You know where you want to go: Los Angeles. You cannot physically see Los Angeles until you are almost there, but you have faith, confidence, and belief that you are on the right path.

Life is like a river. What would happen if you tried to paddle upstream? How far would you get by paddling against the current? You would wind up tired, frustrated, and disappointed. Paddling against the current is like setting a goal while never having determined what plans needed to be made or what steps you needed to take to achieve it.

Unfortunately, most people don't even realize that there is a river of life. The river exists between your two ears, and the destination is what you would like to achieve. It is *your* destination, not that of anyone else. However, the actual journey of your life is the joy that your experiences bring you while traveling down the river. The destination is only the possible end product of the trip.

The next year, I was named Chiropractor of the Year. I also received the highest award that the Parker Seminar distributed, which is the Associate Lecturer Award. This award had been given to only thirty-two recipients in the fifty years that the seminar existed. As I ascended the dais to receive this award in front of 5,000 colleagues, I looked out and realized it was not the physical award in my hand that was the prize. The journey that had brought me here was the real award!

Once you know where you want to go, you might as well enjoy the ride. In many cases, other people or circumstances will try to dictate how you go. Take heed! They are not in control of your life, you are. Your mind is the navigator and your actions are the movement of the boat. The more you learn, the more informed your decisions will be.

What do you really want? How badly do you want it? Are you fighting the current or are you navigating your boat down the river? Are you learning from your mistakes? Do you attempt to overcome challenges or do you let obstacles throw you off course? Remember, the only thing you have total control over is what you think and how you think it. Now, right now, is the only time that you have to improve your life. Do you have faith in yourself or do you listen to other people who may be too afraid to row their own boat? Do you blend into the crowd or do you lead?

Remember Colonel Sanders, the founder of Kentucky Fried Chicken? He dared to market his recipe because he believed it was the best fried chicken anyone had ever tasted. Originally, he marketed that recipe to 1,009 potential buyers. (By the way, he started this effort when he was sixty-five years old.) All of these buyers told him he was just a dreamer. By the year 2000, there was not a city in the United States with a population of over 10,000 that did not have KFC in their town. Who's the dreamer now? *I hope it's you!*

Things to Think About

If you want to be able to more easily negotiate the obstacles along the way to your goals, perform this exercise over and over until you have mastered it. It is a great technique for improving your self-esteem.

- Sit in a quiet place and relax.
- Remember a time when you had thought of a project and then accomplished it. I would like you to picture that scene as vividly as you can. Make sure you include what you saw, heard, tasted, felt, and smelled at the accomplishment of this project.
- In your mind's eye, recount all of the steps that were required for the accomplishment of this project. Notice the obstacles you had to overcome for this accomplishment.

Finally, congratulate yourself on your success!

Football

Once upon a time, there was a very important football game between Nebraska and Florida State.

The Nebraska team was practicing hard and preparing for this game of games. The coaches advised the players to psych themselves to the max. They told the players to hit hard, move the ball, win the game, and then celebrate after.

One of the reserve players came up to the head coach and asked to be excused from practice due to an emergency. The coach realized that the chance of this young man playing in that day's game were between slim and none, so without hesitation, the coach allowed it. The player thanked the coach and left. The coach basically forgot about him and continued the practice.

Finally, the big game was on. After the psychological prep of getting up for the game, the team mood was at a fevered pitch. The young man had returned from his emergency. The coach told him to get into his uniform and get out on the field for the game. The reserve player asked the coach if he could play today. (In the last four years, he had yet to participate in a game.) The coach was taken somewhat aback, but he noticed something different about the young man. So, the coach decided to let him go on the field for the kickoff. However, he also instructed him not to touch the ball under *any* circumstances.

As luck would have it, Nebraska won the toss and chose to receive the ball first. The players took the field. The ball was placed carefully on the tee. Just as the ball was kicked, the kid stepped in front of the obvious kick returner. The coach went crazy! Not only did the kid touch the ball, but he also caught it and was running with it! As the coach tried to contain his anger, he could barely believe his eyes when the kid ran ninety yards for a touchdown! The coach (being the wise person he is) decided to leave this young man in the game.

At the end of the game, Nebraska had won. The outstanding contributor was clearly the reserve player. After the game, the coach asked for a word with his new star. The young man entered the office and the coach says: "Son, you may not have the talent to make it in the NFL, but today you performed like the finest athlete I have ever seen. What happened?" The young man answers: "Remember that I introduced you to my dad a few years ago at Parents Day?" The coach says: "Yes, I do. He's a fine gentleman." The young man asks: "Do you also remember that my father is blind?" The coach answers: "Yes, I do." Then, the young man confides that while he was home that day his father had died. (That was the emergency.) The coach was shocked to hear of the young man's loss and offered his condolences. The young man smiled: "The reason that I played so well today was that this was the first day my dad ever saw me play football!"

Remember, always be nice to people. Care *for* them, and *about* them. From my experience, if you help enough people get what they want, you will surely get what you want. At the end of the day, the coach got his win! I'm confident that you will, too.

Things to Think About

Who inspires you?
- Make a list of three people that inspire you.
- Take the best qualities from each of them, and try to incorporate those qualities into your life.

With mentors to guide you in the right direction and the knowledge that you could not fail, what changes would you make in your life?

Like Attracts Like

We live in a vibrating world. All around us, we see evidence of vibration resonance. This means that everything we see, hear, or feel is a vibration in nature. Have you ever sat next to someone that you had never met before and felt a connection with him or her? Most of us have had this happen to them.

As a cantor for the past fifteen years, I have had many memorable experiences. For me, the most joyous of all occasions are weddings. They are usually beautiful and romantic. One can literally see and feel the love between the couple. As you observe two people looking into each other's eyes, you can truly believe that they are on the same vibration plane.

A few years ago, I was called upon to perform a commitment ceremony between two gentlemen. (They had previously interviewed several clergy and turned all of them down.) On a beautiful spring day, I met with these two individuals. One of them was a two-time Emmy-Award-winning producer, and the other was a well-known name in the entertainment field. The three of us sat and talked for approximately an hour to discuss their ideas for the ceremony. During the entire time, I was absolutely fascinated by the amount of pure affection that the two of them displayed toward one another. It was truly inspiring to see the obvious love they had for each other. By the end of the interview, this special couple had asked me to perform their ceremony.

I was really looking forward to the wedding day. I had never officiated at a same-sex commitment ceremony before. The day finally came, and I arrived with my wife at the couple's choice of venue, an incredibly beautiful mansion. There were about one hundred guests. The two of them had decorated everything, from the driveway to the pool to the gazebo where we were going to stand. They had choreographed every step of the ceremony, which lasted about twenty minutes. As I stood with them under the gazebo, I could literally feel the love. Without a doubt, it was one of the most emotional and uplifting ceremonies that I have ever performed. In all honesty, it was perfect!

When two people connect, they are in vibrational concert with one another. Have you ever been to a music concert and the base guitar was literally vibrating through your body? This is called sympathetic vibrations because you are in the same vibrational plane as the base guitar. Two human beings can come together in exactly same way. Listen to all the eHarmony and Match ads on television! When you find someone who vibrates on your vibrational plane, you have literally found your match. However, vibrations are not limited to age or gender. I hope that you are fortunate to vibrate in concert with most of your family.

To further understand the vibration concept, think of all of the friends that were close to you at one time and have since become estranged. What occurred was literally a change in the vibration pattern of either one or both of you. Keep in mind the saying: *People that are like each other, like each other!*

Things to Think About

If you perform these exercises on a consistent basis, your so-called vibration antenna will become more attuned.

- The next time you go to a meeting, just walk around and observe everybody. Make special note of people that are leaning toward one another or are making really good eye contact with one another. These are the people who are in a vibration alignment with each other.
- Now try this with an outside group, one with which you do not normally work or socialize. Just stand there among them. At that moment, how do you feel? You should feel a different vibration because you are not involved with this group.

Good luck with this. It can be a lot of fun!

Ralph

"You can't row someone across the river without getting there yourself," according to a wise old Indian chief.

Most professionals in the healing arts have chosen their occupations because they truly want to help people. In my experience, sometimes the best help that such a professional can offer is more mental than physical.

During my years of practice, I have come across many different types of people, ranging from longshoremen to corporate executives; and from homemakers to college professors. Some of these patients were incredibly polite and some were quite the opposite. (You could never predict which ones would behave which way!) One of my favorite people was a gentleman named Ralph.

Ralph worked on the back end of the garbage truck for more than twenty years. He loved his job almost as much as he loved his alcohol. He had a beautiful family, including a wife and three children. I was fortunate enough to treat Ralph and his entire family. It was a real hoot because Ralph was, to say the least, colorful!

On one occasion, Ralph came into the office complaining of neck and shoulder pain. I asked him what he might have done to cause this type of condition. He told me that he remembers stumbling out of one of the local bars and falling face down on the curb. He also remembered getting up, readjusting his nose, and going home. I saw him three days after this incident, and his injured nose still seemed to cover most of his face! The prudent thing to do was to send him to get urgent medical care. So, Ralph went to the hospital, had his nose set, and came back. After that day, I adjusted him a few times. After each session, he said he felt terrific.

This sort of situation occurred quite frequently with Ralph.

Members of his family and I had frank discussions among us over their concerns for his health. Unfortunately, their concerns turned out to be well founded when a large mass was located in his large intestine. The doctors determined that the mass was cancerous. Ralph underwent an operation, and for two years, he seemed to be doing well. Then, the doctors discovered that the cancer had spread. His prognosis was terminal.

The family contacted me and told me the news. I was understandably very upset. I explained that I may not be able to improve Ralph's condition, but I was sure that I could help him by lifting his spirits. They thanked me for my concern and told me that they would contact me if the need arose.

Approximately three months later, Ralph's family contacted me. They asked if I would treat Ralph again. He arrived at the office about sixty pounds lighter. His heavily bearded face was gaunt and his eyes were sunken. He walked in without saying a word and was ushered into one of the rooms. I greeted him, but his response was less than enthusiastic. He apparently had no idea why he was there, because he had been told that nothing could help him anymore because he was going to die. I found it hard to respond to that. As he was getting on the adjusting table, he just looked at me with a steely gaze. Knowing that I could not use any force on this man, I just laid him on chiropractic wedges to balance out his hips.

Have you ever been in a situation where you just instinctively knew what you were supposed to do? On my chiropractic table was a man who was going to pass away relatively quickly. I came to the conclusion that the only other comfort that I could give Ralph was to lightly massage his spine while telling him as many dirty jokes as I could possibly remember! After that day, he came to see me three times a week for two months. Each time, all I did was put wedges under his hips and tell him dirty jokes! During these last appointments, he never said a word.

One never expects to hear that someone you cared for passed

away. The news of Ralph's passing came to us via a telephone call from his wife. She asked if I would come to the wake. I answered yes without hesitation. At the wake, his entire family came up to me and told me that, although Ralph never said a word to me, they knew he really enjoyed his visits more than anything. They said that he would talk about them for the two days in between each visit, and even cracked a smile a few times while recalling my jokes.

The purpose of any healing arts practice is to make people better. It was clear to me that the one thing that Ralph needed, which I could give him, was humor!

Have you ever had a time in your life when just a kind word or gesture made you feel better? I am sure that you have had such an experience. Ralph knew that the end was near and wanted some distraction from that realization. My sessions with him provided enough mental relief to make the rest of his life a little bit easier. Caring for somebody's feelings is a wonderful thing.

Remember what the Indian chief said: "You can't row somebody across the river without getting there yourself." I sincerely believe that Ralph's pain was eased a little bit by what we did for him in his last days. What joy it brings to help somebody in need!

Things to Think About

Would you like to become a better listener and a better person? Do these exercises on a consistent basis.

- For one week, try to add an encouraging word in your conversations. As long as you mean it, this could be as simple as: "Have a great day!"
- For a more complex exercise, sit down with somebody who needs to talk and listen to his or her situation. As you listen, make sure you do it with both ears. Listen intently, without trying to make sense of what is said or how you will reply, until the person finishes the thought.

You have two ears and one mouth: You should listen twice as much as you speak!

SECTION SEVEN

Goals

"The significance of a man is not in what he attains, but in what he longs to attain."

Kahlil Gibran
Lebanese-American Artist, Poet and Writer
Author of *The Prophet*

Goals

The more you tell a *negative* story, the easier it is to tell, and the more believable it will become. Is that the kind of message you want to give yourself? You cannot tell a story one way and expect it to turn out a different way. This just does not make any sense.

It has been proven by a myriad of psychological disciplines that you talk to yourself at a rate of approximately twenty words to two hundred words per minute. This is called internal dialogue or self-talk. The majority of self-talk has a negative connotation. On the other hand, when given the opportunity to choose between a positive or negative outcome, your brain will always choose the *positive* outcome!

The unconscious mind does not understand a negative command. A good example is to think of the color blue. Got the picture? Good. Now I'd like you to *not think* of the color blue. What color comes to mind? I'm sure it was blue. When you say to your friend: "Don't forget to come over tonight," you are actually telling them: "Forget to come over tonight."

We can play a psychological game with our unconscious mind to get what we want. Ever heard the saying: "Fake it till you make it."? How about the words: "Act as if...."? What are these sayings encouraging you to do? They are encouraging you to assume a posture. An effective posture will use all five senses to create an image. This is psychological brainwashing! As you transform your entire physiology, you also change the vibration plane. Now add the component of positive thought, and you have literally created a *new you*. Are you interested in improving the current you? I hope so.

In 1905, Wallace D. Waddles wrote a book called *The Science of Getting Rich*. This book promotes the idea of psychologically transforming your thoughts from negative to positive. In other words, what you think about the most is what you get! When you assume a different posture (physiological) and add positive-self talk, you increase the chances of changing the pattern. This sounds really easy. However, to practice this on a consistent basis is to literally re-educate your brain.

After all, your brain has been around for as long as you have. Some "ruts" or patterns are very deeply ingrained. It is foolish for anyone to assume that by making a drastic change quickly that one would get drastically changed lasting results. This is evident when people go on a crash diet and lose a lot of weight. They are understandably thrilled. Nonetheless, six months later, they have usually returned to their original weight. The reason is that they did not change the internal representation (how they think). The more deeply rooted the pattern, the longer time it will take for it to improve. If you are consistent in your zest for change, you will see definite improvement within a short period of time. Notice that I did not say *huge* improvements. So, keep the faith, and keep on keeping on!

In developing your new goal-setting techniques, be aware of your surroundings. As you become more comfortable with these techniques, you will notice more evidence of positive change all around you. It may be as ordinary as a colleague brightening your day by buying lunch or as extraordinary as a chance encounter with a mastermind who propels you to greater achievements.

"If you can see it and believe it, you can achieve it," is undoubtedly true. The operative word here is *believe.* In your attempt to achieve your goals, your beliefs are much more important than your knowledge. In other words that are often heard: "Your attitude is more important than your aptitude." It is *belief* that drives the engine.

A former classmate of mine has truly "gifted hands." He was a great adjuster. He was also one of those people who just did not believe in himself. At our graduation, he earned several awards for adjusting. You would think that he would do very well in practice.

Unfortunately, the opposite was true. Without the advantage of self-confidence, he became the dispatcher for an oil company. Belief rules!

My journey of finding the right method for goal setting has taken me from the traditional to the most esoteric. Traditional goal-setting techniques incorporate a statement of intent, a timeframe, action steps, and verification of the goal. The new generation of goal setting incorporates the use of emotion. The format changed from repetition of statements to creating more of a story. This format utilizes emotion and imagery to help make the intended goal more appealing and achievable. By incorporating imagery, which is right-brain dominant, the goal becomes a whole-brain exercise rather than just an intellectual or left-brain exercise.

In this author's opinion, traditional goal-setting techniques are floored. Just keep your mind open and judge for yourself. As discussed before, the undirected brain will usually think negatively. However, when given the choice between positive and negative, the brain will *always* choose the positive. Belief is the catalyst that makes the difference between achievement and failure of the goal. If that small voice inside your head has any doubt, the achievement of your goal is in jeopardy. All the brain needs is a little doubt, and thoughts can turn negative and ugly.

Your choice of words on paper is important, but the words that you hear in your head are much more important than a beautifully written goal statement. You could include all sorts of descriptive language, but your goals will come to naught if you say them without conviction (emotion) and that "small voice" is not in concert with what you're saying to yourself. If you are consciously saying, "Yes, yes, yes," but your inner voice is saying, "No, no, no," you are in conflict.

So, the ability to make a goal come true is not only dependent on the words we use, but also on the emotion we put behind the words. Nonetheless, the words themselves must be believable. Traditional phrasing such as "I am" or "I see" may not produce the proper image while phrases like "in the process of" or "it's easy to see" seem to make the statement more believable to the unconscious mind. That small voice in your head can't argue with the claim: "I am in the process of being a millionaire." Remember, belief rules!

Timeframes always bothered me because they put pressure into completing the task. I thought I was supposed to enjoy the process, as opposed to getting stressed out by getting finished by a certain time. Sometimes it is better to want to do rather than have to do. That kind of stress or pressure is counterproductive. Having to get something done in a specific time can lead to mental miscalculation. You should keep your eye on the prize at all times, but attempt to relax during the process. The brain works best when relaxed. If you can really get into the total experience of working toward a goal, no timeframe is needed because you are already there! Time just has to catch up with you!

To become totally immersed in your goal, utilize all five senses. Remember, you can see it, hear it, taste it, feel it, and smell it. This method puts you in the moment and causes your conscious and unconscious mind to believe the goal to be true. This is a most powerful technique. If practiced on a consistent basis, this technique will get you to your goals faster than most other techniques out there.

How does the technique work? For example, you may not know what you truly want, but you surely know exactly what you don't want. By exploring what we do not want, we open the internal avenues of communication with your brain (it's the way the brain wants to think). Ask yourself why you *do not* want this to happen. Then, imagine what your achieved goal would look like, how it would feel, how it would smell, how it would taste, and the sounds you would hear if it *did* happen.

Once you have identified the parts you do not want to happen, go point for point, and change each negative aspect to a positive aspect.

This process gives your brain a choice. Again, when given the choice between positive and negative, the brain always takes the positive. Once you have identified the positive characteristics, formulate a scene incorporating all five senses, and float into it. This is a new you: What it looks like, sounds like, tastes like, feels like and smells like to have achieved your goal. This method uses the end product (what you what to achieve) as the driving force. When the end product is imagined this vividly, the path becomes clear.

Let's demonstrate how to use this method. Take the act of getting up in the morning. Having been very comfortable in their beds, many people wake up tired, stiff, and grumpy. Can you relate to this?

Using the new goal-setting method that was described earlier, first you would identify all of the parameters of getting up in the morning that you do not like. Write them down:

I don't want to move from this comfortable bed.

I'm still tired.

I'm really stiff and sore.

I feel really grumpy.

As you consider each statement, you need to draw upon your experience and recreate how it feels to be ousted from bed, tired, stiff, and grumpy. This part of the process is stroking the brain with negativity. Remember, both words and feelings are really important here. The more you can truly jump into this picture, the more dynamic the potential change will be. Write down key phrases to tell yourself that will instill a negative mood. Now that you have personified this truly yucky and unhealthy feeling, slap yourself in the face (metaphorically)!

Now, turn each of the negative statements into vivid details of what you truly want. Each positive statement has to indicate one of the ways you would ideally like to feel in this situation. Write those statements down.

I can't wait to start the day.

I feel enthusiastic.

I am flexible and feel great.

I am truly happy.

Now, draw from your life experiences again, and recreate getting into those positive moments. You use the same process for both sides of the equation. By doing the process in the same way, you now have two sides of the same coin. Again, we are at the point of choice.

The challenge here is to get into the feeling and enthusiasm that the positive responses give you. Once you have incorporated your five senses into this intensely positive situation, rejoice in the moment. Picture yourself waking up in the morning, getting out of bed quickly and easily, and feeling truly happy and enthusiastic. Mentally rehearse this scene several times during the day. The object is to be able to see that scene and achieve that feeling of accomplishment. Over a period of time, this feeling will supersede any negativity. Soon, getting up in the morning will be a joy rather than the dreaded routine of just another day.

When you give your brain an alternate choice to negativity, the brain will always choose the right path. Therefore, by having rehearsed the positive side of the situation, your chances of accomplishment have greatly increased. From now on, each time you think of your goal, you will get that really good feeling. This feeling leads to belief, which leads to achievement. Mastering this method can lead to success and the journey to get there is definitely challenging, stimulating, and exciting!

Things to Think About

Is there something in your life that you would like to change? When you look at your bank account, does the bottom line depress you? Is there some other aspect of your life that you would like to improve? If you are not where or who you want to be, you and your mind may be stuck in a negative mode.

- After you have re-read the last chapter, decide on a goal or outcome you want to achieve. Identify exactly *what you want* by first formulating *what you truly do not want* to happen in this situation or event.
- Gather extensive information about the positive and negative aspects of this outcome.
- Make contrasting lists. First list the negative aspect on the left. On the right side of the page, list the positive side.
- Look at both sides. Which one looks, sounds, tastes, feels, and smells better?
- Construct a scene incorporating all the positive aspects that would result once the outcome is complete. Now make that scene bigger, brighter and closer to you. Live it in your imagination!

Practice this process often until that feeling is constant within you. When you do this, you are truly becoming the person you want you be and are on your way to achieving your goals.

Epilogue

After I was finished writing, my wife and I had a conversation about this book. I commented that I had written a lot of material in six months. She reminded me that I had been writing this book in my head for about thirty-five years!

It is true that I've wanted to put my thoughts on paper for a long time. However, the time just did not seem right... until now.

Since you are reading this book, you must feel that the time is also right for you. Perhaps it is the time to change. Perhaps it is the time to take chances. Perhaps it is time to have a new outlook on life.

You have encountered a perfect opportunity to change what you need to change, in order to be what you truly want to be. Trust that all is possible.

Harris

About the Author

A learned man with life experience, Dr. Harris Cohen treated patients in his private chiropractic office for more than twenty-five years. During this time, Dr. Cohen listened carefully to their health issues. In the process, he observed that his patients inundated themselves with negative messages that prevented them from moving forward in their lives and in their health. He began speaking to them about "negotiating" with themselves to reach the right choices that would provide them a happier and healthier lifestyle.

In addition to his thriving practice, his professional career included: assistant professor of clinical sciences-University of Bridgeport, assistant professor of clinical sciences-New York Chiropractic College, lecturer-Suffolk County Police Department, pharmaceutical representative-Ross Laboratories, teacher-junior high and high school biology and chemistry, cantor-Mastic Beach Hebrew Center, and teacher-Yeshiva of Suffolk County.

Dr. Cohen has also had an impressive formal education with the following degrees: doctor of chiropractic-New York Chiropractic College, master of science in human sciences-C.W. Post College, and bachelor of arts in biology-Hartwick College. In addition, he has been trained in communications with advanced certificates in neurolinguistic programming. He has also been certified as an EMT, AEMT, and CPR instructor/trainer.

Dr. Cohen is the recipient of numerous honors and awards including: Dean's List-Hartwick College and New York Chiropractic College, President's Award-New York Chiropractic College, Clinic Award and Director Assistance Award-New York Chiropractic College. He has also been named Chiropractor of the Year and received the Parker Associate Lecturer Award from Parker Chiropractic School.

Dr. Cohen lives on the East End of Long Island with his wife Corinne, who he considers the love of his life.

CPSIA information can be obtained at www.ICGtesting.com
Printed in the USA
BVOW071539130412

287633BV00001B/2/P